Ten Pound Pom

Terry Parker

First published by Busybird Publishing 2021

Copyright © 2021 Terry Parker

Paperback: 978-1-922465-39-9
Ebook: 978-1-922465-41-2

This work is copyright. Apart from any use permitted under the Copyright Act 1968, no part of this publication may be reproduced, stored in a retrieval system or transmitted in any form or by any means, electronic, mechanical, photocopying, recording or otherwise, without the prior written permission of Terry Parker.

Cover Image: Destination Australia by Marjory Parker
Cover & typesetting: Busybird Publishing

Busybird Publishing
2/118 Para Road
Montmorency, Victoria
Australia 3094
www.busybird.com.au

Dedicated to my family.

My father, Arthur Parker, who had the courage to bring us from the cold to the warmth.

My mother, Marjory Parker who had the patience and love to keep the family together.

My brother, Colin and sister, Judith, who have shared much of my journey.

The surprise packet, Raymond, a brother to be proud of.

And of course, my brilliant wife, Lesley.

Contents

Introduction	i
1. Yorkshire the 1950s	1
2. Bilton	7
3. Tears, Fears and Canings	23
4. Heavens to Betsy	41
5. Not the Expected Holiday Break	49
6. Secondary School (The Hero in Tears)	55
7. Whatever Happened to Sheila Whitfield?	63
8. Ten Pound Poms	67
9. Where Shall We Go?	71
10. Finsbury Hostel	75
11. A Town Called Elizabeth	83
12. To the Desert	89
13. Woomera	93
14. From Desert to the Sea	107
15. Naval College	111
16. University	123
17. Fleet Manoeuvres	127
18. Epilogue	135
Appendix A: What is a Ten Pound Pom?	137
Appendix B: The Barber Line	141
Appendix C: A Brief History of Yorkshire	145
Appendix D: A Brief History of Woomera	153

Introduction

This book is written by a British Migrant, who as a boy of 14, travelled from rural England with his family to settle in Australia. It is a personal account of an early life in North Yorkshire, the family's emigration to Australia in 1964 and my subsequent experience as a young adult in South Australia and New South Wales. The events happened as stated, although the memories may be tinged with a sense of nostalgia.

I have only recently started to think about my heritage and early life. I am not a person to look backwards but as I have previously written several snippets about my past. I thought it worthwhile to join them together, hence this book.

Before we engage in this journey, I feel obliged to declare my allegiances.

On arrival in Australia, I decided that I was an Australian and have maintained that as my primary loyalty, although my thickish Yorkshire accent has often led others to think differently. For example, throughout my Australian Naval College days, I was known as 'Pom' and subjected to many, mostly jovial, taunts. A favourite jibe was to cast doubt on English hygiene.

'How do you get a pom out of a car? Throw in a cake of soap' (To put the record straight, I have showered at least daily for my entire life in Australia).

What took our family from the insular community of my childhood to Australia? Australia was seen as a land of opportunity and my mother and father wanted their three children to have that opportunity. Secondly, and possibly more importantly, my father, a restless soul, wanted to travel.

He had served as a Royal Marine during the second world war and when he returned to Yorkshire, little had changed. There were some minor inconveniences. For example, food rationing did not finish in the UK until July 1954 when I was four and a half. The effects of the war continued well into the 1950s and beyond. These privations had little effect as Yorkshire folk were very used to 'going without'. Quite a contrast to today's consumer-led society.

Sure, the horses had been replaced by tractors and the towns sold a wider range of product, even French produce, but most villagers rarely ventured into town and bought their basic needs from the local grocer and butcher.

My father met my mother on return from service in 1946. I was born in December 1949, 18 months after they married. A couple of weeks later and I would then have been brought into the world in the next decade. I therefore qualify as a post war 'baby boomer'.

My Dad left the Marines just before I was born and became a Fireman, firstly in keeping fires alight on steam train boilers and later putting out fires as a member of the West Riding of Yorkshire Fire Brigade. Mum became a stay-at-home mum looking after three energetic children, as was the way in those days.

It is important to reiterate that, thanks to my mother and father, I never felt deprived or subservient. I had an idyllic childhood and would not swap it for 'all the tea in China'(a cliché that goes back to the tea trade of the 19th century). Yorkshire folk loved their tea and it was the first thing considered in times of strife.

Introduction

But Australia was the land of opportunity so Dad packed his bags and his three children and in 1964, we headed for Australia. It seems strange today but the only thing we knew about Australia was extracted from *The Reader's Digest World Atlas*. As you will read later, we had no idea where we would end up and in fact Dad changed his mind about our final destination because he knew of somebody who was related to our next-door neighbour.

There are three significant episodes documented in the book. Finsbury Migrant Hostel tested our determination to stay. It was violent, unhygienic, dirty and impossible to leave until enough money was raised for rent elsewhere (Dad had about ten pounds when we arrived in Australia).

Our escape was to Woomera in the South Australian desert and what a privilege it was to live there. I finished school in Woomera and was accepted into the Royal Australian Naval College and further dramatic character building.

If nothing else, this epistle has enabled me to re-evaluate almost forgotten experiences that, in a sense, crafted my character and outlook on the world. In this sense, as the hackneyed phrase goes, 'Everybody has a book in them'.

It surprised me to find in my research that the places and stories of my younger days are much written about. For example, the disused railway tunnel where I overcame my fear of the dark is now quite famous; Woomera where my family lived for eight years is well-documented. Ten Pound Poms like my family have made a significant contribution to Australian life.

Terry Parker

19 November 2020

SIGNATURE OF PARENT, GUARDIAN OR OTHER PERSON HAVING CHARGE OR CONTROL :—

M E Parker

JH 244500

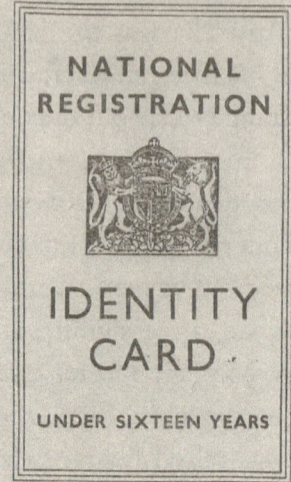

NATIONAL REGISTRATION

IDENTITY CARD

UNDER SIXTEEN YEARS

NUMBER: M.K.Q.C. 287 :   SURNAME: PARKER

CHRISTIAN NAMES (First only in full): TERENCE N

FULL POSTAL ADDRESS: 208 SKIPTON ROAD HARROGATE   KNA

THIS IDENTITY CARD IS VALID UNTIL 17th DECEMBER 1965 ONLY

CHANGES OF ADDRESS. No entry except by National Registration Officer, to whom removal must be notified.

REMOVED TO (Full Postal Address): 31 HALSTEAD ROAD. HARROGATE. KN17.

REMOVED TO (Full Postal Address): 51, BACHELOR GARDENS, HARROGATE. KNA.

REMOVED TO (Full Postal Address):

REMOVED TO (Full Postal Address):

FOR OFFICIAL ENTRY ONLY. ANY OTHER ENTRY OR ANY ALTERATION, MARKING OR ERASURE IS PUNISHABLE BY A FINE OR IMPRISONMENT OR BOTH.

NOTICE. The parent, guardian or other person having charge of the person to whom this Card relates must sign his or her own name in the first vacant space on the back.

The person having charge is responsible for the custody and production, when required, of this Identity Card and for the notification of any change of address of the person to whom it relates.

Within seven days after the 16th birthday of the person to whom this Card relates that person must produce it at the local National Registration Office for the issue of a new Card.

1
Yorkshire the 1950s

With a population as big as Scotland's and an area half the size of Belgium, Yorkshire is almost a country in itself. It has its own flag, its own dialect, its own unique culture and Yorkshire Pudding.

In fact, Yorkshire Pudding is an integral part of the culture. In the 1950s, social status was not bestowed by money or luxury but by the quality of your Yorkshire pudding. This is perhaps a slight overstatement but it signifies the uniqueness of the culture.

Yorkshire is the largest county in England but it is by no means crowded and encompasses some of the most isolated areas in England, particularly in the North.

The people of North Yorkshire are stereotyped as bloody-minded, stoic and minimalistic, and this was certainly true of the people in my early life. You only spoke when you had something to say, said it with a minimum of fuss, and then assumed it to be fact.

On Ilkla Moor Baht 'at, the national anthem, reflects this attitude. It is short in words, many of which would not be understood by southerners, and fatalistically describes life as sickness, death, subsumption by the earth and recreation as a duck on the dinner table. Thus, the last verse, 'Then we would ave eaten thee.'

There were two major occupations in the county, mining in the South and farming in the North and it is these arduous occupations that encapsulate the Yorkshire way.

It is perhaps unnecessary to expound on the rigours of coal mining. The perception of streets of grey stone terrace houses leading to the pithead where grimy miners work 12 hours a day 'down t' pit' have been well-documented, so I will leave it to those more competent than I, to illustrate.

The Yorkshire Dales, where I grew up, are steeped in history dating back to medieval times and before. Vikings occupied the north for centuries and many villages and rivers derive their names from this period. The Norse word 'dalr' (dale), means river and the word for Yorkshire's many crags and hills; the Fells, is also from a Norse word meaning mountain.

Small hamlets, some dating back over a thousand years stand aside the winding rivers that give the dales names such as Airedale, Wharfedale, Swale dale, Nidderdale, Arkengarth dale, Bishopdale, Clap dale, Coverdale, Kingsdale, Litton dale, Langstroth dale, Ray dale, and Walden dale to name but a few.

Medieval farmsteads are dotted across the Yorkshire Dales. And centuries old dry-stone walls form intricate patterns that mark boundaries of long forgotten farm holdings. A survey conducted in 1988 recorded almost 5,000 miles of dry-stone walls in North Yorkshire.

The Fells are high and barren landscape moorlands that surround the dales. The purple moorland is dotted with hardy sheep that have to withstand severe winters of minus temperatures, sleet, snow and ferocious winds.

The wildness of the Yorkshire Dales, isolated from much of Britain, finally ended in the nineteenth century when railways were built to cross the county supporting the wool trade which still features as the major industry in North Yorkshire. Several large viaducts that seem to enhance rather than spoil the countryside, still stand to celebrate the coming of the railway. Many of the railway routes were cancelled in the 1980s but the railways still play an important part in Yorkshire culture and certainly in my childhood, as testified in several parts of the book.

Wool extracted from sheep on the high moors, drove the economy in the nineteenth century and still goes on today as a major contributor. In the valleys, mixed farming was the major source of livelihood.

The climate contributes significantly to the Yorkshire way. In winter, deep snow congregates on the moors and it is not unusual for farmers to have to dig out sheep from snow drifts. Winter can be extremely cold — even in the valleys — and sleet, rain and snow can fall for many weeks. The usually short summer reveals some of the most beautiful scenery in the world. The difference between the soft summer and harsh winter could be contrasted to that of the Australian hinterland.

It has been said by students of the 1950s and 1960s that the industrial north recovered slowly from the war and many Yorkshire folk were obliged to live frugally. We were used to living frugally but we never thought of ourselves as poor. It was just the way we were in the dales of North Yorkshire. In the farming land where I lived, nothing was wasted. We recycled waste vegetable matter long before it became popular and yes, we had to eat everything on our plate or miss out the next meal. As young children, we had everything we needed.

'Waste not, want not' was a popular cliché of the time.

We were what we were, and our only sense of class difference was for those outsiders from 'down south.'

Most Yorkshire inhabitants thought of it as a working-class county. Economic hardship and hard work have been a major factor for many Yorkshire families. And this created a unique subculture that is still today, epitomised as fiercely independent to the point of exclusivity. You were from Yorkshire first and England second. To illustrate the point, you had to be born in Yorkshire to play for the County Cricket Team until fairly recently.

The Wars of the Roses were still felt strongly in Yorkshire even though members of the two sides, The House of York, and the House of Lancaster, were really southerners with 'Estates' in Yorkshire and Lancashire.

Even the language is unique. The dialect in the dales, which unfortunately has largely disappeared, is almost unrecognisable as English. My granddad spoke in this fashion and was often difficult to understand, even to a fellow Yorkshire man. In fact, each village had its own grammatical idiosyncrasies and in days of yore, your speech defined your village of origin.

As previously stated, they did not waste anything in Yorkshire, even words, so Granddad rarely spoke when at home but when he did, you listened (even if you did not understand a word). The Yorkshire slang is composed of a few old English words — some unique to each area — that have been whittled down to their simplest form and then denuded of conjunctions, prepositions, and other unnecessary grammatical frills. You would not hear a dales man say, 'Would you please close the door?' He would say, 'Put wood in t' hole.'

The outside world, apart from a few camping trips outside of Yorkshire, was largely unknown and we had no pressing desire to know. But dad was a restless soul and wanted to improve himself and/or travel. Mum, his best friend, supported and endured his wanderlust and as a result, we travelled extensively throughout the UK and eventually ended up ten thousand miles away from our home, in Australia.

We were imbued with a very real sense of geographical and cultural isolation, particularly from those down south, that is anywhere south of Yorkshire. We were real Yorkshire folk and proud of it. So,

1. Yorkshire the 1950s

I grew up in a virtual bubble, but not necessarily a bad bubble. We were not troubled by the turbulence of the outside world and if any 'do-gooder' had suggested that we were deprived, we would have strenuously repudiated it (if we could have used such a 'posh' word).

I now realise that growing up in Yorkshire has provided a foundation for my identity and persona.

Dry Stone Walls

Ribble Dale Viaduct

2

Bilton

I grew up in a suburb of the beautiful spa town of Harrogate, the self-proclaimed 'gateway to the Dales' and a health resort for the well-to-do. My family, however, did not hail from the posh end of town and were proudly working class. I correct any misconceptions regarding this by stating that I was born and grew up near 'The Gasworks' a prominent feature of the lower end of town.

Mixed farming was the main industry in Bilton and there were five farms within a kilometre of my home. The farms mainly produced milk but there also were chickens, pigs, and some sheep. The fields also yielded wheat, barley, and other crops — notably turnips — which were very much part of the staple diet. The fields, farms and woods of rural Yorkshire were my early playground and figure fondly in my reminiscences.

I grew up in a community that had no interest in the goings on down south. Atomic bombs, the Iron Curtain, and who happened to be Prime Minister, were of no interest to Yorkshire folk. The goings on at Number 7 and or the fate of Yorkshire sporting teams was paramount. There were few cars and even fewer televisions, and only the rich or adventurous were interested in the world outside.

Bilton is a small village that rates a mention in William the Conqueror's Doomsday Book (value 3 shillings). Bilton was subsumed in the nineteenth century by the larger town of Harrogate. The order of loyalty was for your street first (Bachelor Gardens because of some allotments at the bottom of the road), then Bilton, Harrogate Yorkshire and finally England. You needed a lot of loyalty in those days!

It is a difficult idea to articulate in a world where we may have a less defined allegiance to our city, state, or country but it spoke of community first; a concept that would go well in today's multi-universe. I now appreciate the value of those days and, to be honest, I feel a little sad for the technology mad world of today that has lost those sentiments and experiences.

We lived in a two up, two down semidetached council house that was basic but comfortable. Everything revolved around our local community. Even Harrogate town was only visited for a doctor's appointment or something equally dramatic. The town by the way, was a mere kilometre away.

We went to school or played in the woods and fields that surrounded our house. Life for a primary school kid was simple but never boring and, in many ways, idyllic.

I cannot remember much about my first home. It was a one-bedroom upstairs flat with an external concrete staircase. I remember the staircase because I fell down it several times.

Our second home, the fountainless, 22 Fountains Avenue was rented from the council and was a basic two up, two down configuration. Upstairs, there were two bedrooms and the only bathroom/toilet (with bath but no shower). Downstairs consisted of a lounge room and kitchen; hence 'two up, two down'.

Our third home, 6 Wainfleet Road, also a council house, had a third bedroom (sheer luxury).

The strong community culture was firmly anchored to the past which meant that misdemeanours were roundly punished, and corporal punishment accepted as the norm. Surprisingly, the threat of punishment had little effect on us. As the cliché goes 'You do the crime, you serve the time.'

Some authors paint pictures of horrible beatings and adult cruelty during this period but this is a complete misconception. Punishment was punishment and reward was reward. Pity had no part in our lives. Quite the opposite. We were safe and free, within certain bounds, to live life as we pleased. There was no concept of being abducted by strange men or run over or threatened in any serious way. The rules were not negotiable but simple. We felt no pressure to be successful or famous. That only happened to those kids 'down south'. If we showed signs of academic prowess, it was encouraged but not mandated. If we showed sporting prowess, playing for the Yorkshire Cricket team was the goal.

Not that our lives were without challenge. We attempted many daring physical endeavours, of which the modern child would have no concept.

The Bilton woods that ran alongside the river Nidd were dark and gloomy, owing to the entangled pine trees that formed a light repelling cover over the ground. Bilton Woods were only occasionally visited as it was thought to spawn unknown terrors. I think it was our parents concerned that we might get lost or worse, who planted the idea of danger in our impressionable minds. There was even a report that a nudist camp existed deep in the woods. It might seem innocuous now but our C of E indoctrination defined nudist camps as sources of evil. The woods were defined as out of bounds but most young boys were programmed to push the envelope.

I recall my brother Colin, two years younger than me and an unadulterated show off, climbing a particularly tall pine tree to the very pinnacle. He looked down and waved to the impressed gang below, lost his grip and fell breaking every pine branch on his downward journey before crashing to ground at a fearsome speed. He lay there prone for several minutes as we looked on in trepidation, fearing the worst, before bursting into laughter at our fearful expressions. He had landed on a cushion of pine leaves and was completely unharmed.

In order to access the Bilton Woods, we had to cross the railway line, also out of bounds. The railway line was a source of both wonder and danger.

Five ten-year-old boys stand on the railway line adjacent to the fearsome monolith, The Viaduct, that crosses the Nidd River. There is some trepidation; it is almost 4 o'clock when the gleaming green monster that pulled the north bound pullman train will storm across the viaduct.

A dare has been declared and 'dares' are not optional if a boy wants to maintain his social status.

The short grey trousers, long grey socks, and fair isle jumpers — carefully washed, dried and ironed by proud mothers — are now besmirched by the day's adventures. Mud forms dark brown diagonal flashes on the erstwhile pristine jumpers. The waistband of the grey flannelette long shorts are either hitched up to the belly button or allowed to swirl around the knees depending on the whim of its owner.

The short wavy hair of the boys — carefully combed in the morning until it resembled a well-formed curve — is now tangled by the many briar bushes (called secret hideouts by the boys) and falls from their heads with a will of its own. The most striking feature is the knees. Years of crawling through bushes and climbing trees has transformed the knees from the soft pink of youth to grimy grey; a grey that even Mum's energetic scrubbing cannot erase. It's easy to tell a town kid from a field kid regardless of their appearance or valeting; it's the knees.

The dare is a common one, rush onto the bridge as far as you can just before the train comes and then launch yourself over the parapet onto the steep stony banks of the Nidd valley. Obviously, the furthest wins (if he survives).

2. Bilton

There are tall tales but perhaps not true of one boy, admittedly a secondary school kid, who actually jumped directly into the river from the centre point of the viaduct[1].

This story was discounted even by we impressionable ten-year-olds. After all, the viaduct was over one hundred feet high and surely someone who fell that far would not survive. The most recent 'dare winner' had jumped from a creditable fifty feet but had emerged with significantly bloodied knees after rolling uncontrollably onto the riverbank.

The Pullman's daily transit through our little world was the stuff of dreams. In our little backwater where cars were a rarity, these gleaming green monsters, the fastest steam engines in the world, effortlessly towing ten or more brown and cream carriages, would streak across our play fields. It was a relentless brute force, a majestic beauty that only young boys and railway tragics could appreciate.

On another occasion, we constructed a rope swing on a tree overlooking a small pond in Uncle Charlie's bottom field. The idea was merely to climb the tree to a place where the tree forked and swing out over the pond, releasing your grip before the apex of the swing so that you landed safely on the other side of the pond. BUT there was a fork some metres higher up that only the brave would attempt. The swinger (no not that kind) was in free fall for a perhaps two metres before the rope took up the slack. Not exactly skydiving and completely bereft of any safety rules.

The dare was voiced and there was no way any self-respecting kid could refuse a dare. It occurred to me as I climbed to the top of the tree, that I had never actually seen anybody jump from this position. But, what the heck. If I jumped, hero status would be conferred on me until the next dare. Unfortunately, the rope was old and my weight was more than its breaking strain, and I ended up flat on my back in the pond. Bungee jumping is for wimps.

---

1. Nowadays, it is a walking track, but there are plans to rebuild the railway from Harrogate to Ripon. A railway is better.

Good came out of it though as a young lady who called herself 'Susannah' was sympathetic to my plight, if not my prowess, and undertook to become my girlfriend. She even pushed my mum's bike which I had been riding, back to my home whilst I hobbled along behind her.

You can assume, rightly so, that I was incredibly naive. Girls were a complete and terrifying mystery, particularly as the stirrings of puberty contributed to my discomfort when faced with the prospect of meeting a girl. I was unsure what girlfriend meant at the age of around ten, but Susan, sorry, Susannah, apparently did. It did not require physical contact, other than the occasional holding of hands when nobody was looking. It did, however, involve the writing of passionate letters covered in scent and 'SWALK' sealed with a loving kiss, written on the envelope.

Some weeks later I was ditched for a more mature youth. But all was not lost, I was handed over to the scoutmaster's daughter, Sheila Burdon, and the writing of letters continued (not by me). Oh! The fickleness of the opposite sex!!!

In these days of entertainment overload, instant information and worldwide travel, the dales of North Yorkshire seem quaint and somehow ethereal, but we had very few boundaries outside the strict school and family environments.

We had chores from an early age, but these intrusions were manageable if you were smart enough to at least appear to be compliant, and we spent much of our time inventing new games or stories and as my mum would say, 'Making a mischief of ourselves'. The world held very few fears. We wandered where we wished without fear of adult intrusion. Our young, imaginative minds and unlimited access to fields and woods were all we needed for entertainment.

My granddad worked on Ingram's Farm, where Dobbin, the Shire horse, would graze beneath a large oak tree. Dobbin had pulled a plough in his early days and had been granted early retirement. Dobbin was unperturbed when two likely lads, my cousin, Trevor, and me, jumped onto his back and leapt into the lofty eyrie of the oak tree's mighty tangled branches. The tree is still there today in the front yard of a brick veneer town house which itself stands in the middle of a housing development. Is this irony or progress? How the place of my boyhood has changed.

Time has also significantly altered Bilton's financial status and today, the town of Harrogate is one of the most sought-after areas to live in the United Kingdom. It is unlikely that the environment of our youth could be replicated today. It may be an old-fashioned perspective, but not all changes are for the better.

Most people in our community were long term residents and rarely moved to a new house or changed their routine or lifestyle. My father's parents for example, lived in 51 Bachelor Gardens, at the bottom of our street, all their married lives. Uncle Charlie, who shall appear in this story later on, had lived and worked with his wife, Aunt Ada, at Knox Farm since he had left the Army after World War I. Knox Farm was just up the road from our house and one of my favourite places. Uncle Charlie's daughter, Nancy, my dad's favourite cousin, lived next door to my grandparents, separated by a farm gate that led to the 'back field'. Dad's sister lived next door to us, Uncle Eric next to my school, Bilton Endowed, 200 yards away. Uncle Wilf also lived on Bachelor Gardens. In fact, only one of Dad's five brothers lived outside Bachelor Gardens.

It was probably this closeness and because he had the only car, that allowed my father as the eldest of seven children to visit all the relatives on Christmas Eve to deliver Christmas presents. At each location, he would be offered a glass of Port which was drunk only at Christmas time. He would return home in a very merry mood after these visits

Mum's family, her mother, father, sister, and brother even lived in the same short road, a couple of miles from our house. I have fond memories of Granddad Scott, Mum's dad, ferrying me on his bicycle crossbar to his home at 31 Halstead Road.

At its best, the atmosphere was nurturing and supportive; at its worst, it was an emotional and financial straight jacket. Youngsters in the area were expected to grow up as farm labourers or workmen, or if they showed promise, tradesmen. As far as I know, my cousin Trevor and I, were the first university graduates in the area.

Strangers were unknown and it took the locals some time to accept the new residents who moved into posh new bungalows that had been built in the area (much to the annoyance of the locals). It is not that Bachelor Gardens people were unfriendly, quite the opposite, they were very hospitable, but they definitely did not like change.

I can recall two occasions that exemplify this introspective attitude. The dislike for anything non-English or more particularly, French, was demonstrated by my Uncle Eric, who, in 1979 had not seen me for fifteen years. I remember that he rushed out from his very ordinary council house, not to welcome a long-lost nephew as I thought, but to order me to remove my French manufactured motor car from the front of his house.

Later that day I met our ex-next-door neighbour, Mrs. Cooksey, in the Bilton Working Man's Club. She was the only one to see us off when we left for Australia and had babysat us kids on many occasions. 'How wonderful to see you our Terry' was not in her vocabulary although, 'our Terry' was. All I got was a shrug and a grunt.

Having said that, when the formalities (read grunts) had finished, she was able to recount every birthday, significant event, and some not-so-significant occurrences in great detail. It reminds me of the famous last line from the film *Babe*. The pig, Babe, has just won the most prestigious sheepdog trial against all odds. The farmer's last words are, 'That'll do pig.' In Yorkshire this would be considered unnecessarily wordy and 'over the top'. The laconic Aussie rural culture has a lot in common with the Yorkshire understatement.

Knox Farm was built around 1650 and figured significantly in our lives and I recall many wonderful days there with my cousin Trevor.

2. Bilton

It wasn't really a farm anymore as Uncle Charlie, my great uncle, had leased most of the fields and restricted his farming activities to chickens. The farm buildings were clustered around the seventeenth century farmhouse which I am sure had a dirt floor when I was young, and was surrounded by dry, stone walls and fields as far as you could see. The outbuildings were typical: a dairy complete with stone trough, a mistal (milking shed), stables converted to use as garages, hen coups on stilts to keep out the weasels and foxes, and various other sheds.

The chicken coup later became the scene of a reproduction of World War II's Great Escape as re-enacted by Trevor, my cousin, my brother Colin, and me. Colin, the youngest, was posted as lookout while Trevor and I crept under the chicken house and started digging a tunnel which would lead to freedom. In fact, the tunnel was about 2 metres long and merely led to the middle of the field.

Of course, we would have drilled a hole in the chicken coup to make our escape even more realistic except for the fact that Uncle Charlie would be a bit cranky if he found a hole in the floor, and even worse, we would have to remove many years of chicken poo to get to the floor.

Paradoxically, another hut, where newborn chickens were kept, was the location of a real failed escape of which I still bear the scar.

Newborn chickens were hatched under a large heat lamp located in the middle of a timber slatted hut. The hut was situated across the driveway from the entrance to the farmhouse and was explicitly classified as out of bounds. Uncle Charlie had quite rightly forbidden entry, fearing that the over exuberance that personified his grandson and grandnephew would terrify the newborn chicks. Unfortunately, 'no' was interpreted by us as, 'not right now'.

The door was padlocked but Trevor and I managed to stack some old boxes against the wall and thus, gain entry via the only window which was about half a metre wide and two metres above the ground. I still remember the sight of about twenty newborn chicks scrabbling about under the very warm lamp. A beautiful sight that both of us really appreciated.

Unfortunately, the chicks did not and, as Uncle Charlie had surmised, the chickens were not overly enamoured by our presence and a concerted physical and audible ruckus ensued. Uncle Charlie, alerted by the noise, rushed from the door of the farmhouse which was surprising as I had never before (or since) seen him rush anywhere.

From inside the hut, we heard the rattling of the padlock. Trevor who was next to the window, climbed out and jumped to the ground outside. I was not so lucky and to avoid detection, I dived headlong out of the window breaking the glass with my knee.

Realising that the game was up, the two of us stood forlornly outside the farmhouse fearing the mother of all reprimands, or even worse, some humiliating physical punishment. Uncle Charlie, normally a good-natured chap, was black with fury and fair enough as we had seriously threatened his livelihood.

Head bowed, we awaited our fate, but Uncle Charlie's wrath was halted by his wife, Aunt Ada, who had seen the gash in my knee which was deep enough to expose a fair amount of bone.

Strangely enough, there was little blood but the extent of the damage was clear. Punishment would have to wait, and after some ministrations from Aunt Ada, I was rushed to hospital in my dad's motorcycle and sidecar, where several stitches were inserted (not in the sidecar). The incident was forgotten but the scar remains to remind me of my errant youth.

My cousin Trevor and I, both imaginative lads, built tunnels beneath disused hen houses, built a running track using miles of string, a cross country bicycle raceway and ran the world's most unsuccessful transport company.

Tunnels, for some reason, were high on our construction agenda. We built two types of tunnel. The simplest were trenches covered with bits of fencing and then covered with dirt. The reason for their clandestine nature was never really discussed, after all they were secret tunnels. Obviously, their secrecy would have been compromised if a purpose had been articulated.

The second type of tunnel, as I have already mentioned, resembled a World War II escape tunnel and started under the hen house and went... well I cannot say that it actually went anywhere because that is a secret.

Hens were pretty dominant in those days, or at least their eggs and poo were, and any construction required a significant amount of poo removal. It goes without saying that our mothers were not impressed after a day of tunnel building.

I well remember the bicycle course. I was the only one to traverse it because Trevor did not have a bike. It was an old black ladies' bike, which may at one time have belonged to my mother. I broke the track record on many occasions. In fact, on every lap.

The second racetrack was our version of an athletics field consisting of miles of sisal (string) tied to bits of wood that we scavenged from a disused storeroom. Its purpose was to ensure that the runners stayed on track so to speak. We invited the best runners in Bilton. We only knew two: Stuart Henderson and his brother Stephen who had competed in the regional school's athletics carnival and were therefore considered very quick.

Trevor did not do sport so Stuart and I, bounded by miles of sisal, rotated round the track to replicate the athletic heroes of yore. I was running the marathon, Stuart, the hundred yards dash which somehow turned out to be about the same distance. We both won our events despite suffering enormous setbacks. Mine was an imaginary broken leg suffered when my evil rival organised a nobbling halfway through the event. Oh, the simplicity of heroes and villains.

The transport company was a grand scheme. Our 'fleet' consisted of two wheelbarrows, a wooden box with wheels attached (a bogie) and an old pram whose origin was shrouded in mystery. We were more interested in the vehicles than a marketing plan and had to bribe my sister with sweets (lollies) just to get business. I think we transported her from our house to the farm and she complained bitterly that the wheelbarrow was extremely uncomfortable and had dirtied her dress. You just cannot please some people.

Trevor was the brains of the outfit, he is a year older than me, but I was a willing accomplice to some very hair brained escapades.

We exploded cow pats with fireworks to simulate the effect of an atomic bomb, and exploded a model of the Houses of Parliament which Trevor had built, to celebrate the demise of Guy Fawkes. We may have been naive but I think we were happy.

The origin of Bonfire Night goes back to an infamous attempt to blow up the houses of Parliament by a Catholic dissident, Guy Fawkes. He, and twelve co-conspirators, spent months planning to blow up King James I of England during the opening of Parliament on November 5, 1605.

Their assassination attempt was foiled the night before when Fawkes was discovered lurking in a cellar below the House of Lords next to thirty-six barrels of gunpowder. Londoners immediately began lighting bonfires in celebration that the plot had failed, and a few months later Parliament declared November 5 a public day of thanksgiving. Guy Fawkes Day, also known as Bonfire Night, has been around in one form or another ever since.

Speaking of fireworks, other than Uncle Charlie's anger, Bonfire Night was the highlight of the social calendar and involved the whole community.

The local kids would spend many hours dragging dead wood from all over the district in an effort to build the biggest and best ever bonfire. Fireworks, marshmallows and sausages were the pre cursor to the grand bonfire lighting. The whole neighbourhood attended without exception. The bonfire was often honeycombed with tunnels for no particular reason and were crowned with an effigy of Guy Fawkes manufactured by the local women.

Bonfire night was a boy's version of ecstasy. We had recognition for building the best bonfire ever, permission to light fireworks (particularly two-penny bangers), and were able to partake in a wondrous array of cakes, sausage rolls and the like.

The bonfire itself, was around 4 metres wide and high. It would be ceremonially lit by the senior men and we would all gather round, usually in freezing cold, and just admire the fire and fireworks. I still remember the names: Catherine wheels, Rockets and Mount Vesuvius. It was all on a small scale. The fireworks budget was measured in shillings, not millions of dollars. I remember looking at the reflections of fire in the eyes of the enraptured spectators.

I thought that the most enjoyable bit was scouring the local woods for wood. Gangs of primary school kids would pull huge (to us) branches, sometimes for a distance in excess of a kilometre to the 'back field' owned by Uncle Charlie, just behind my grandma's house and next to Mrs. Prest's attractive Apple Orchard. But that is a story of intrigue, treachery and criminal intent that deserves its own paragraph.

The Bonfire Night bonfires were a symbol of pride for each local community. Although it was impossible to judge the biggest bonfire, it was assumed that ours was always the best.

The importance of the Bonfire in the local community, was exemplified by the reaction when our archrivals, The Fountains Avenue Gang, stole into the back field two days before bonfire night and burnt our bonfire to the ground. To the outsider, this may seem like a minor issue, but this was the major item on the community's social calendar and required an actual bonfire as its centre piece.

I will not say that the adults took over, as bonfire night was built and enjoyed with children in mind. They did, however, metaphorically, pick us up, dust us off and propel us in the direction of rebuilding our precious artefact. The exhausting and time-consuming task of wood collection was accelerated when several grown-ups joined in. The horse had perhaps bolted but our parents created a security roster for the back field to ensure that the Fountains Avenue Gang could no more destroy our effort.

At 5pm on Bonfire Night we were still dragging fuel to the bonfire from any potential stockpile, including logs that had previously been allocated to winter hearths.

The kids would normally have engaged in Mischief Night. Mischief Night occurred the night before bonfire night. Doors were randomly knocked on, honey was smeared on doorknobs, front doors were tied together and various substances poured through letter boxes to name a few of the mischievous pranks. I have no idea as to the origins of this practice. It seems a strange custom in these enlightened years.

There was no Mischief Night in Bachelor Gardens that year as the rebuilding continued unabated. The result was the best bonfire night ever. I hated those unnamed scoundrels from Fountains Avenue, an area we considered to be at the bottom of the socio-economic pecking order, but their action galvanised the community in a way that was uplifting and meaningful.

I mentioned Mrs Prest's apple orchard earlier. It was one of the orchards that was fair game to the local lads. Apple Scrumping was another forbidden activity. The pre-harvesting of apples by the local kids (scrumping) was an acknowledged past time in autumn and was considered by most of the adults as fair game because most of them had engaged in the same pastime in their youth. Technically, we were stealing apples, but our adolescent brains considered it to be just one of the things you did as a kid. Orchards were rated in terms of danger; the headmaster's orchard was top of the list and tales of derring do were usually slightly exaggerated.

Apple raiding may seem fairly innocuous, but the risk of being caught was significant and exposure could affect a young kid's reputation (a hero to the kids, a villain to the adults). As far as I remember, all the kids did it, even goody-goody cousin Trevor. We were once chased all the way from the allotments at the bottom of Bachelor Gardens to Hare's Farm, a distance of approximately one mile by an old man with a stick. Eventually, we escaped into a familiar copse in a high state of excitement. The stick, from memory, rivalled that of Bill Sykes in *Oliver Twist*, but may in fact have been a walking aid. Ironically, the apples that we stole were Crab Apples, small, hard as rock, bitter and completely inedible.

Trevor, always the entrepreneur, and I concocted a scheme to sell the proceeds of our adventures as Toffee Apples to the local kids. We built a fire in the woods and tried to melt Highland toffee[2] over our stock of stolen apples. There were two minor problems. The apples which had been buried in a secret stash for some weeks, were going off, and Highland Toffee could only be melted by the direct application of a powerful blow torch, which of course we did not have. In the end, we couldn't make the toffee apples and finished up with some rotten apples and inedible burnt toffee.

Grandma Parker's name was Isabella but she was always called Bella. She was a fearsome character to us kids, except for brother Colin who she had adopted as her favourite. 51 Bachelor Gardens was her unchallengeable domain. Her word, or more specifically her copper stick, was more dominant than any mad dictator. When he was home, Granddad occupied the only single seat sofa by the fire and rarely stirred from it. Grandma ruled the roost.

Granddad Parker worked hard as a farmhand, literally from dawn to dusk on Ingram's farm. At 5am, rain or shine, he set off for the farm with Jip, his faithful collie, and a small metal milk urn, returning at 6pm with an urn full of milk. His chair, next to the fire, was sacrosanct and even Grandma would not break its mystical boundary. Grandad's return, typical of Yorkshire folk, involved no excessive verbiage. In fact, not a sound was uttered. He would walk into the laundry, Bella allowed no footwear in the house, take off his boots (or booits in Yorkshire parlance), walk to his chair by the fire, put on his slippers, light his pipe and wait for his dinner. Jip took up her station under the table in the impossible hope of catching some throw away food during dinner.

You may surmise — correctly — that Harry Parker, my grandfather, worked hard during his working day, but Jip seemed to do most of the work. She could open the farmyard gate, round up the milking cows and shepherd them into their assigned stalls in the milking shed. If Granddad could have worked out a way for Jip to

---

2. Highland toffee was purchasable from Mrs. Mires shop in Bachelor Gardens for two pence and displayed a portrait of a Highland Bull with Huge Horns. Hammers were more effective than teeth in breaking it up, although some sissies were thought to suck it into submission.

attach and remove the milk teats, his physical presence would not have been required.

In later life, my dad told me that Grandma Parker had a beautiful soprano voice. I never heard her sing unfortunately, but perhaps her fearsome reputation masked a sensitive inner soul.

I suppose philosophically that my adolescence was lived in a bubble, but what a lovely bubble. It featured real stuff, not bank accounts, action toys or self-proclaimed importance, but things such as camaraderie, right and wrong, and relationships with real people.

Psychologists say that we manipulate memories for our own benefit but what do they know. I remember the good and the bad with equal nostalgia and I swear every word in this tale is absolutely, unquestionably, undeniably, indubitably factful.

3

Tears, Fears and Canings

I have already mentioned that my childhood was pretty idyllic but there were boundaries which, when overstepped, could result in more pain than pleasure. Most punishments were far more effective in prospect than in the punishment itself and were rarely administered. Punishments at school ranged from a smack with a ruler to a formal caning, an example of which is chronicled in the next paragraph. The faint of heart should skip it.

As stated, children were rarely caned and then only the very errant boys suffered the ignominy of a caning. Although, I do remember a group of small boys gathering around an older boy who had suffered from the cane, eagerly listening for the gory details of the pain suffered. Girls were never physically punished and regardless of the sin were only ever given detentions. The girls were called by their Christian name and treated with respect. The boys were called by their surname and always suspected of planning a new mischief. They were correspondingly controlled with more vigour for good reason.

I attended Bilton Endowed School founded by two Christian benefactors in 1793. It was a small school, some four classes and less than forty students. My father had attended the same school and had acquired a reputation for mischief. He was, and still is, a reactionary free spirit which throughout his school days and subsequent career earned him more punishment than reward. His less than perfect disciplinary record preceded him and I, as his eldest child, was, I suppose, expected to do good to make up for his wayward reputation.

There are memories too numerous to chronicle but I will indulge myself and mention a few.

The school had no assembly hall as such but two of the classrooms were separated by a glass partition that could be pulled aside to provide a reasonably large space. I recall our annual Christmas play which was performed in this arena. Desks had been pushed together to form a temporary and unstable stage. The enthusiastic parentage awaited their little heroes to display their acting ability.

The play opened as Joseph, played by yours truly, appeared on the desks, banged his staff (sorry stage) and announced that Mary and he would go to Bethlehem. As with most ten-year-olds, I walked along the desks to centre stage, surveyed the audience in true 'Olivier' fashion and banged my staff onto the desk. Unfortunately, in my enthusiasm, I banged the staff between two desks and lost control of it. It rolled noisily along the floor under the 'stage'. My first soliloquy was delivered to this diversion as the teaching staff ventured under the desks in an effort to retrieve it. I cannot remember too much about the rest of the play except that for some reason Baby Jesus, performed by one of the junior girls' dolls, was lost, which created yet another break in the proceedings. Oh well! What do you expect from amateur drama?

The second incident, which caused me great suffering was the first day of second term in Miss Dickinson's class. For some unknown reason, Miss Dickenson had arranged the class desks in a U shape and announced that the students would seat in merit order around the classroom. Now, even at six or seven, I thought I was ok at academic studies and expected my name to be called out in the first few. But it wasn't! Oh well, middle of the class is ok. Names were being called but no Terry Parker. As the students took their seats leaving a dwindling group of unclassified kids, I was suddenly faced with the possibility that I would be near to the bottom of the class. Indeed, my name was the last called out. I remember forcing back tears. The ignominy of it, and more particularly, the shame of facing my parents. I was devastated. I stood for a fair while contemplating my failure before shuffling to my subservient position at the bottom of the class. I wanted to cry but I couldn't, not in front of all these kids that I had known all my life.

Ok, you have probably guessed that Miss Dickinson read the list out from bottom to top, but I was too naïve to realise it.

It speaks to the unvarying nature of our community that my second-grade teacher, Miss Dickenson, also taught my father. I once suffered the ruler across the knuckles administered by Miss Dickinson, more in memory of my father's escapades than for any fault on my part. It goes without saying that my father had transgressed several times under Miss Dickinson's rigorous tutelage.

Remembering Miss Dickinson and her brother, the local Anglican Minister for the area, reminds me not only of the unchanging archaic nature of our community but also of its stability and its security. My father and I were both birthed by the same midwife, Miss Dawson, and were taught by the same teacher. Midwives and female teachers did not seem to marry in those days.

My one-off punishment was nothing compared to the humiliation suffered by another boy from Bilton Endowed. Alan Alsop was a serial miscreant from the class below. The headmaster, Mr. Brown, decided to make an example of him after many offences including truancy, theft, sticking pencils into a girl's bottom and numerous other crimes. Caning was considered too brutal for girls and younger students, and only the senior class boys were called to witness punishment in the senior classroom.

Alsop was arraigned in front of the class whilst Mr. Brown prepared. I had always thought of the headmaster as rather meek and mild. He was smaller than most of the ten-year-old senior boys, bald with rimless glasses and reputedly dominated by Mrs. Brown who taught the class below. It was the only time that I saw him remove his tweed jacket (with the leather elbow inserts) revealing a white shirt with arm clips, presumably to keep his cuffs away from the ink wells. The clips were removed, and the sleeves rolled up. The cane was extracted from its secret location and Mr. Brown took a few practice swings.

In the meantime, the victim, for such he was, stood facing the class with a smirk on his face. I think that he had anticipated the occasion and stuffed a workbook down his pants in true schoolboy fashion. But Mr. Brown was an educated caner and went for the hands.

This changed Alsop's expression to one of fear as he was asked to extend his hands in readiness for punishment. At that moment I wanted to be anywhere but in that classroom and I think Alan did as well but I won't dwell on the actual punishment, 'six of the best', other than to say that each of the best was a fearsome act, exercised with all the force and leverage that the headmaster could muster.

I can still remember the whirring of the cane as it descended with great pace. I am not sure what happened to Alan Alsop, but I wish him well as much for the humiliation he suffered, as the punishment itself. Ironically, this type of punishment by humiliation was repeated many years later at Naval College but I will leave that for a later chapter.

On the home front, corporal punishment was also an accepted practice but was usually carried out with far less ceremony with a leather belt or – in Grandma Parker's case – a copper stick. I never saw it used in anger, but my father assures me it was well used in his day. For us, I think it was employed as a mere threat, although I do

3. Tears, Fears and Canings

remember Grandma chasing me around the back yard brandishing the fearsome stick[3].

I should explain that the stick was not metal but made of wood and used to stir clothes in the for-runner of the washing machine. The other kind of fear, equally potent, was the fear of witches, devils, and other nefarious hobgoblins. It seemed very real in that anachronistic bubbled world, steeped in the cultures of the past. Stories of immortal dogs, witches that predicted the end of the world and ghosts of past evils, were woven into the fabric of life. The occult was never overtly recognised and rarely acknowledged by adults but the stories were handed down over generations.

I was particularly susceptible to these stories, having been blessed and cursed with an active imagination. The few examples I offer seem tame and unrealistic, but they were very real to an impressionable child.

Knaresborough, a market town, three miles from Harrogate, was home to a fifteenth century mystic, called Mother Shipton who of course lived in a cave in the woods nearby. She made many predictions, one of which was the end of the world which would occur when Knaresborough's low bridge collapsed for the third time. It has collapsed twice since the fifteenth century and is probably the best maintained bridge in the area. The pub, which stands next to the bridge is even called 'The End of the World'.

I was in the Boy Scouts. My first scout camp at Castle Howard was a disaster as I got very homesick and it rained continuously for the first three days, as only it can in North Yorkshire. The food, which we cooked on open fires, was usually over or under cooked adding to my sense of despondency. I remember we cooked a dish

---

3. For the uninitiated, a copper was a metal vessel, used to wash clothes. The water was heated via a wood fire underneath (replaced by a gas element in later times). A block of washing soap (washing soap was coarser and much cheaper than body soap) was scraped into the water, the dirty clothes added, and the whole lot stirred with your weapon of choice, usually a sturdy wooden rod. An optional wringer could be added so that the water could be squeezed out of the clothes on exit. Wringers claimed many inquisitive fingers in their rollers.

called Beef Hash, which was a mixture of cold burnt mash potatoes and tinned corned beef. The mere mention of Beef Hash still evokes a sense of nausea. We were always seemed to be wet and cold which definitely dampened our spirits (another pun).

Rain would often inundate the tent and our sleeping bags were inundated with water on several occasions. Needless to say, this does not make for a good night's sleep. In the morning, we were obliged to dress in our cold wet clothes, go outside to our cold wet outdoor kitchen and try to light a fire, not always successfully, with wet wood and matches. Cornflakes and milk became the order of the day on these occasions, but at least the milk didn't go off easily. After a day's wet outdoor activities, we would return to our camp, attempt to light a campfire and, if unsuccessful, retire to our wet tent and sleeping bags.

We were a tough lot! I suppose that, in some ways, these very real hardships resulted in a tolerance for most things and a genuine respect for the good things of life.

But I digress yet again. I had risen to the exalted rank of patrol leader of the six person 'Eagle' patrol, which meant that I could supervise rather than do, and I got the best (driest) possie in the tent at night.

Two patrols from the 1st Bilton Troop and one scout leader were camping on Blubberhouses Moor[4]. The moor is in fact on top of a blue tinged hill some few miles away from the hamlet of Blubberhouses (nothing to do with whales). The rain had cleared for once and we were clustered around the campfire after the mandatory scout community singing, 'gilli something'. We were listening to a local historian tell stories of the area. His last and most enduring story concerned an ancient wizard and his experiments to produce eternal life.

---

4. Blubberhouses is a small village and civil parish located in the Washburn Valley in the borough of Harrogate in North Yorkshire. It is situated to the south of the Yorkshire Dales national park, and to the north of a Roman road. The name is said to originate from the Saxon word for 'blue mountain'.

3. Tears, Fears and Canings

I understand witches. Hooked nose, warts, a pointy hat, and a broom to get around. Despatching spells and prophesies huddled around a boiling pot. But wizards? Wizards seemed rather mild compared to the aura of witches but that opinion changed one night on the Yorkshire Moors.

Why do witches have cats and wizards dogs? Apart from Merlin, I didn't know of any other wizards. They seemed to have only two pastimes which they always failed to achieve: alchemy and eternal life

Anyway, this wizard lived in the fifteenth century and he was one of the eternal life kind. Just like all other wizards, he had developed a potion that he thought could achieve his goal. He was a cautious wizard and decided to try the potion on his dog, which of course was grey and blackish and nondescript as are all wizards' dogs.

At first, the experiment went quite well, and the dog had lived well passed its normal lifespan. But there were some unforeseen side effects (drum roll please). The dog grew and continued to grow and had grown to the size of a small horse. It also developed a rather vicious temper and a taste for live meat. Perhaps most animals would be a bit grumpy if they had to live with a boring old wizard well past their normal lifespan.

The dog took to roaming the moor at night and the local villagers reported seeing it howling at the full moon filling the valley with a mournful anguished cry. It had huge saucer-like eyes and was seated on a black rock silhouetted against the moon. Naturally on such occasions, black storm clouds scudded across a troubled foreboding sky. Ok, I had to let my penchant for clichés run free just once.

Sheep were found dead and horribly mutilated the day after the dog sightings. Naturally, the dog was blamed, and the locals forced the wizard to chain it at night to a rock adjacent to the wizard's house. The wizard's ego was dented and subsequently he withdrew to his laboratory and was rarely seen by the villagers. The villagers forgot about him and his dog for several years.

The reader can probably guess the rest of the story, but I will tell it anyway. Several years later the dog appeared yet again on top of the rock, silhouetted against the moon with black storm clouds scudding across a troubled foreboding sky and, of course, the sheep got mutilated again. The dog had escaped from its chains, dispensed with the wizard, and resumed terrorising the local district. Just how the dog dispensed with the wizard is a matter of taste, pun intended.

It's a tough life being a sheep on the Yorkshire moors. Snow, freezing temperatures, and grass so tough that you have to chew it for half an hour, then wait for mutilation in one way or another. All you want is a quiet life eating grass and following your friends around and what happens?

Stories abounded of villagers being chased by a huge tooth gnashing animal with two glowing, saucer-like eyes the size of a medium sized horse. The villagers, however, were unconcerned, apart from the loss of sheep, as local knowledge reassured them that magic could not cross water. After all, there was always an old rickety wooden bridge in the vicinity.

Anyway, the story goes that quite unexpectedly, the sheep ceased to be mutilated, a welcome relief for them, and there were no more dog sightings. That is of course, as the local historian told it, until a few weeks before our camping expedition, when the ghostly howls and silhouetted rock topping glimpses started again.

I have mentioned Alan Alsop previously and, whilst he had matured somewhat since the caning, he still exuded a mischievous demeanour. He was a member of my patrol and had an idea to scare the other patrol. The idea was so engaging that we immediately agreed to execute his plan.

The patrols took turns to travel through the black night, along a sheep path to the local tarn (small lake) for our nightly ablutions and teeth cleaning. Our patrol had the first turn the following night and, instead of returning to the campsite, four of us climbed a three-metre black rock conveniently located next to the tarn. At the top of the rock, one of our number stood up and held two torches at around the height of the eyes of a fierce horse-sized mutilator. Two other members of the patrol crouched behind him to resemble the body and I, hidden from view, prepared my most ferocious howl.

In due course the Sparrow patrol (actually, this was our put down name for them as their real patrol name was the Kestrel patrol) appeared at the tarn and started their nightly routine. At a given signal, the torches were turned on and my most blood curdling howl pierced the silent blackness.

We thought to frighten them but initially their only reaction was to remain transfixed in the middle of whatever ablution they were doing. Were they up to our rather amateurish ruse? No, they were literally frozen in terror. After what seemed a very long time, one of their number was able to partly overcome his numbing terror and then slowly, not to antagonise the monstrosity, rose to his feet and started to edge his way back down the path accelerating as he went until he disappeared round the rock at an Olympic pace. This roused the other members of the patrol and they followed suit at a pace far greater than they would normally be able to muster, with flailing arms and terrified screams. In the aftermath of this little escapade, I learnt that they had careered down the path, ran past the bemused scoutmaster and were only stopped a few hundred yards from the village.

The power of a dark night and a terrible ghost story cannot be underestimated. I later recounted 'the big dog story' many times, minus our prank, and managed to scare quite a number of innocents. Oh, shame on me!

I had my own share of terror. I remember walking past an old stone house, most of which had crumbled to the ground. It was purported that a crazy old woman had died there — obviously from a broken heart — and that she still haunted the grounds. Have you ever tried to run past somewhere whilst attempting to replicate a studied walk?

One of the scariest things that I ever attempted involved my cousin Trevor and a long disused railway tunnel. The narrow-gauge line was built to supply coke to the local gas works. It started from the main railway line at Bilton Crossing where mainline goods trains would transfer the coke to the narrow-gauge train, and it continued some three miles to the gasworks. The dominant feature of the line was an awfully long dark tunnel of about one kilometre in length which opened into the gasworks. The tunnel entrance was a forbidding railway culvert just wide enough for the train and several metres below the ground. Both ends of the tunnel had been bricked up but some of the bricks had been loosened so that a smallish boy could remove some of the bricks and squeeze into the tunnel. The tunnel entrance itself, blackened by years of soot and disuse, seemed almost surreal. I remember the silence of the place as Trevor and I contemplated whether there was any way that we could escape from our mutual dare. But a dare is a dare and we were determined to conquer the tunnel and its ghosts.

We commenced our journey in a cautious and falsely ebullient manner, skiting about past experiences, but when the tunnel took a turn and the light at the tunnel entrance disappeared, a more sombre but still determined mood prevailed. We had not brought torches as that would be 'sissy' and literally felt our way along the tunnel sides. I was on the edge of panic but to retreat would have been cowardly and cowardice was the ultimate sin to a pre-testeronic Yorkshire lad. I focussed on putting one foot nervously in front of the other.

I think Trevor felt the same way but neither of us were prepared to admit fear. After what appeared an eternity, we realised that we could just make out the wall of the tunnel, which signalled that we were nearing the other end. Our journey to the gasworks end of the tunnel finished with disappointment. An iron grill barred the exit and could not be removed without some kind of explosive device, which of course we did not have. Although I do recall that Trevor had a notion to return at a later date to see if it could be overcome.

We had no choice. We had to return through the blackness to exit the tunnel. The return, however, was fairly uneventful as we had become accustomed to the spider webs and occasional deep pit-like holes in the track. I think though, that we did the walk-run thing again.

The experience and our ability to overcome the fear was character building to say the least.

22 Fountains Avenue - My second home
(Aunty Joan lived the other side of the drainpipe)[5]

---

5. This two-up two-down concrete rendered Wimpey council houses were built in thousands in the 1950s provide low cost housing. The **Wimpey** No-fines House was a construction method and series of house designs produced by the George **Wimpey** company and intended for mass-production of social housing for families, developed under the Ministry of Works post-World War II Emergency Factory Made programme. 'No-fines' refers to the type of concrete used - concrete with no fine aggregates.

3. Tears, Fears and Canings

Knox Farm showing the Mistal, Dairy and Farmhouse
(The shed, housing the new-born chicks, was opposite to the farmhouse)

Bilton Endowed School Circa 1956

1932 Jowett 7 Like 'Betsy' but in better condition

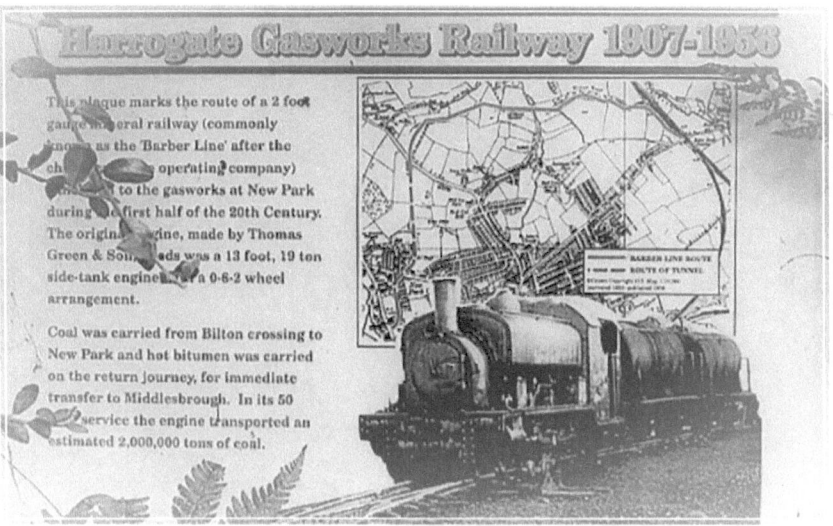

The Barber Line

The Tunnel Entrance

Family Pictures

Above: Dad (right) and best Friend Frank

Left: Mum (right) and Aunty Kathleen in Blackpool

3. Tears, Fears and Canings

Above: The Three Siblings with Cousin Roy[6]

Right: The Parker Children Circa 1957

---
6. Colin broke his arm when he jumped off our coal bunker. He used the caste as a weapon to defeat the street bully, Mickey Todd.

4
Heavens to Betsy

My father was and is a restless soul with a wanderlust, piqued by service in Europe and the Far East as a Royal Marine during World War II. As a result, Arthur and Marjory and their three children sometimes ventured outside Yorkshire on their camping holidays, a tendency noted by most people in our village of Bilton, as bordering on insanity.

'What's wrong with seaside at Bridlington (50 miles away) and if thou wants a real treat, hop over to Lancashire and see't Blackpool illuminations'? As previously mentioned, Yorkshire folk don't indulge in the luxury and superfluity of prepositions and conjunctions. They are a Spartan lot.

Thinking now about my father and his exploits, I remember some scary moments with motor vehicles on our wide-ranging holidays. (We even went as far as Cornwall some 200 miles away). On one occasion, Dad attempted to take 'Betsy', for that was the car's name, up the Sutton Bank, a 2 mile, 1 in 4 climb, that modern cars ascend with ease.

Betsy was a 1932 Jowett with a rated horsepower of 7.0 that Dad had rescued from the New Park Tip. She was wont to splutter and even stop at the most inconvenient times. despite Dad's many ministrations.

There was no thought of motoring steadily up the narrow winding road as Betsy would probably have expired half-way up and caused a significant traffic jam.

'Revs is what we need,' said Dad. 'There is a turn out half-way up. If we can get to that point, well we can work out the rest when we get there.' The turnout was the only place to stop as the road was narrow and did not even have shoulders.

Betsy was old and tired and wielded several horsepower less than the seven HP she was rated for, but Dad had faith. Mum and I were instructed to look out for vehicles going up or coming down the Bank. Dad needed as much room as he could to charge up the bank. The assault started a couple of miles from the hill, the distance needed by Betsy to get to her maximum speed.

'Dad there's a truck coming down and it looks big.'

'Too late now lad, we 're committed.'

On we raced at a speed that made the old car rattle and shake violently.

Up she goes.

'But Dad we are slowing down. Can't you go faster?' Dad had the accelerator pedal down to the floor.

'Dad, do you want us to get out and push?'

But Dad didn't reply. He was focussed on the turn out bay, still 100 yards away, willing Betsy to one more effort.

And then we were there. Only just, as Betsy had slowed to Zimmer frame speed. We pulled in and Betsy let out a huge woosh of steam. We got out, shaken but not stirred. We were used to this as Betsy's radiator leaked more than a Prime Minister's office. She had to cool down for some time as Dad said that we'd crack the head if we put cold water in straight away. After ten minutes or so, Dad decided that she had cooled down sufficiently to fill up the radiator with water that we always carried for just such an event.

Mum said that we should go back down, after all, the view halfway up was almost as good as at the top, but Dad was thinking. There was no question of a run up as the turnout was just a few metres long, but he wasn't going to give up.

'I think we will take it slow this time. The lowest gear on a car and therefore the one with the most torque, is reverse. We will reverse the rest of the way.'

So off we went up the hill at a very unsteady one mile an hour with Dad focusing intensely on the many curves on Sutton Bank as he reversed Betsy up the hill. Attempting this feat in an unreliable and underpowered 1930s car was not easy, particularly as the rear window was not only tiny but, due to its age, almost translucent.

Every now and then Betsy would threaten to stall but Dad, a fire engine driver, would calmly take her out of gear, rev her up and reengage reverse. We were travelling so slowly that even my little sister could have got out and overtaken us. Dad forbade any such suggestion.

'But Dad if we all got out, the car would be much lighter, and we would have a better chance of reaching the top.

This made sense of course, but you do not trifle with Dad when he has his determined face on.

I remember looking out of the windscreen. A jam of cars had formed behind us as we chugged slowly and not too certainly up the hill. The expressions in those vehicles following us ranged from mild humour to utter frustration. After all, they drove vehicles that did not need to reverse up the bank and were manufactured after World War II. I remember looking at their faces and thinking how lucky we were to have such a unique view of the cavalcade of vehicles following us up the hill. Of course, just as Betsy was about to expire, she pulled into parking area at the top of Sutton Bank with a final triumphant gush of steam and an exhausted rattle.

We had to suffer another ten-minute wait for her to cool off whilst several of the occupants of the following cars balefully stared at us for delaying their erstwhile smooth journey. They didn't look dangerous, but it was extremely embarrassing to be stared at in such a demeaning fashion.

Thankfully, Dad was concentrating on reviving Betsy, otherwise he might have 'shirt fronted' the other drivers. Dad is like that. He had achieved an almost impossible feat by getting Betsy up the mountain and he was not going to let others spoil his triumph.

One RAF type, complete with handlebar moustache and MG sports car, ambled over to look at Betsy.

'Could I look under the bonnet? How did you get that up here anyway?'

Dad was delighted that the gentleman was interested. He lifted the bonnet, propped it up with a stick which we kept in the car and started to explain the workings of a pre-war motorcar

'934CC twin horizontally opposed cylinders, but the best and biggest thing in this car and what got us up the hill, is the flywheel. It takes a while to get her going but once the flywheel gets up to speed, you almost don't need the engine. Thankfully!'

At least one driver had admired Dad's ingenuity in getting us to the top and Dad was, as they say in Yorkshire 'Right chuffed.'

'Don't delay Dad. Fill up Betsy's radiator and let's get out of here.'

Eventually, Betsy was re-watered, and we sheepishly spluttered out of the parking area on our way to Whitby, our intended destination.

Unfortunately, Betsy had to be written off after 'a lady driver' had careered round a corner in a 'modern car' and smashed into Betsy, who was stationary at the time. Dad was injured; I think he broke his thumb; but Dad was philosophical about the incident.

'Those modern cars are no good in a smash. They are based on sub-frames instead of proper a solid chassis. Reckon Betsy saved my life.'

We weren't sure what sub frames were, but dad had pronounced Betsy's obituary and that was that.

Mum said he was lucky to be alive and that ended any speculation on our part regarding chassis versus sub-frames. I reckon today, 2020, Betsy would be worth a lot of money, but in those days she was only good for scrap.

4. Heavens to Betsy

We had no insurance, so I was expecting another exploration of the New Park Tip. I think Mum put her foot down as the next car we had was manufactured post World War II. Just.

There were other occasions of similar ilk. We returned home from the Blackpool Illuminations (a colossal 80 miles away) with only the handbrake to arrest our progress, but I will not bore you with a litany of more driving adventures. I will say to all drivers of modern cars that you don't know what you are missing. The thrill of journeying far from home in a pre-war car, not knowing if you would reach your destination, was an adventure that I loved. Mum had a very different opinion.

Dad and Mum did not have much money. They worked hard, lived in a council house and could not afford to go to restaurants or resorts. You might say that we were economically disadvantaged, but we never felt that way. I know now that we were different from most of the Bilton inhabitants. At least Dad was. Perhaps it was his war time globetrotting or that he had been a surrogate father to his six siblings whilst his father was away on military service. I think that he was an innately restless soul who always wanted to push boundaries. He still is at the age of 94.

So, the staid farming community of Bilton could not understand why we undertook camping holidays way down south in Devon and Cornwall. Why would you want to take your holidays outside Yorkshire? The seaside at Scarborough or Bridlington was as far as most folk would go. Sixty miles was a long way in those days.

Things that happened on these adventurous sojourns became the stuff of legends in our imaginative worlds. On one occasion on another trip across Filey Moor to Whitby, we were travelling in two vehicles as there were four adults and an unspecified number of children.

One vehicle was an ex grocer's van owned by Uncle Ron (my father's brother in law who lived next door to us) which still sported the green and white livery of its previous owner. Our van, a blue well-travelled Austin 8 built in 1948, sported back windows and was, in a way the predecessor of the modern estate wagon.

Each vehicle transported two adults and half a dozen or so kids. I make this point because it was not certain how many and whose children were in each vehicle.

We stopped at a lay-by (turning bay) on top of Whitby moor in a very isolated section of the road. The minors piled out with requests to purchase ice creams from the conveniently placed ice cream van or to attend to a call of nature.

I was one of the latter but as a ten-year-old with mysterious genes flooding through my body, I craved privacy. I struggled through the coarse bushes beside the road and headed down the hill in search of a convenient location. I don't know if my search took me too far down the hill or if I was distracted by some thought or situation, but it was sometime later when I returned to the layby to find it deserted. Even the ice cream van had gone.

In realty my plight was not serious. The road was reasonably well travelled and a ten-year old on his own would certainly attract the attention of passing motorists I was not thinking logically in my panic. I had been abandoned to an uncertain fate and for the first time in my life, (that I will admit to) I dissolved in tears.

I was lucky. The next vehicle to pass the lay-by was a Ford Zephyr police car. I had read about these vehicles; especially hotted up to enable them to catch errant criminals attempting a motorised escape. A popular police serial on the TV at that time was 'Z-Cars'. It starred the famous actor, Brian Blessed, and he had become one of my heroes. A trip in a police car? What a thrill! Of course, not all people would feel the same way.

My sorrow forgotten by this happenstance, I was able to communicate my problem to the two friendly policemen, who undertook to pursue the two children laden vans and restore me to my family.

What a ride! I observed the speedometer reaching well in excess of 70 mph (at least double Betsy's top speed) as we careered around bend after bend before coming across the sluggish vans that had just realised my absence and were turning around to search for me.

I still remember fondly the excitement of the chase and the moors flashing past at speeds well in excess of anything that my Dad's old vehicles could aspire to.

These memorable times reflected a time both free and engaging with a hint of danger that could have caused some significant injury, but 'No pain no gain'.

The family's camping holiday at Langdale Pikes in the Lake District was a typical example of this.

5
Not the Expected Holiday Break

My family was on summer holiday in the Lake District of North West England, camping as usual, and yet again outside our county of Yorkshire. It was the summer of 1962 and I had just turned 11 and was about to embark on my first big school, Harrogate Grammar School.

Langdale Pike is a sharp ragged mountainite, protecting an expansive but almost featureless brown gorse plain. Our little circle of tents was situated on a fairly remote (as remote as you can be in England) camping ground. My imagination saw this as vulnerable to Indian attack. I imagined myself as the hero and decided to climb the mountain to locate the enemy and protect the wagon train below. I had to scale a vertical rock face and several times rocks were dislodged as I slipped and almost fell into the enormous chasm below. Edmund Hillary, the New Zealander who climbed Mount Everest, was my hero so I combined mountaineer with cowboy. Easily done in a childish imagination.

Unfortunately, I had overestimated my mountaineering capability and, although the slope of the modest hill was no more than 45 degrees, I slipped once too often, lost my footing and became a rolling, yelling ball. My momentum was finally halted when I cannoned into our tent, almost destroying it.

My Dad angrily berated me.

'Tents do not grow on trees you know.' A rather meaningless statement to a cowboy/mountaineer and, in any case, tent poles do come from trees

Dad was not sympathetic to my imaginary adventures and banned climbing for the rest of the holiday. He threatened to cancel the holiday if I climbed anything more than into bed. I could have said that this would be difficult as we slept on the ground under blankets (no expensive sleeping bags for us), but discretion is the better part of valour. It did not seem to be the right time to argue semantics with a fuming belligerent adult.

Frustrated and no longer able to play Cowboy or the first man to climb Everest, I scan the horizon for adventure. The only feature of the plain was a stream which split the plain in half. It was fifty-metres wide in eleven-year-old terms but less than three-metres in reality. I could still be an Indian scout, fearlessly leaping across the chasm to rescue the beautiful lady from the wagon train. (The testosterone was only just starting to have an effect.)

'I trot, Indian style across the prairie, effortlessly covering vast tracts of ground as I search for the kidnapped victim. The river comes in view and without altering my rhythmic stride, I leap across its vast emptiness, to land crouched and ready for action on the other side'.

Unfortunately, the width of the stream was significantly more than my leaping capability and I landed clumsily in the middle of the stream injuring my foot as I landed on the stony bottom. The pain was just bearable and nothing was going to stop this hero's mission. I overcame the tribe of Indians holding the damsel hostage, rescued her, and returned triumphantly to camp.

5. Not the Expected Holiday Break

I returned to the camp a hero but oh my foot was hurting and I could feel it swelling in my shoes but heroes show no pain and so I kept my injury to myself. My parents remonstrated with me for missing lunch but did not notice my discomfort.

Minor injuries were quite common in our adventurous little world, but I was to find out later that this was not minor. My little brother, noticing my awkward walk, called me hoppy and my 7-year-old sister just smiled.

Five weeks later, my foot was becoming more painful by the minute, but of course an Indian Scout casts off pain as a slight inconvenience. As the oldest and supposedly most responsible child, I was sent to the post office to post a parcel. My little brother still called me hoppy and my sister still smiled knowingly but I had managed to keep the severity of the injury from my mother and father, though they showed some concern.

'It's nothing Mum. I just have a sore ankle.'

I knew she was not convinced but I stuck to my story and she was obliged to accept my explanation.

In reality, my foot was so sore that I could hardly bear to put it on the ground and I definitely could not put weight on it. My other foot was sore from taking all my weight. I was terrified that I would miss the first day of Grammar school if the true extent of my injury were discovered.

Unfortunately, Aunty Joan was leaving the Post Office as I lent on the wall to recover my composure. I had kept my injury from my parents because I did not want to waste my time at the doctor's, but Aunty Joan's unexpected appearance gave the lie to my condition.

'You do look pale our Terry.' (Yorkshire people are the epitome of understatement and the possessive endearment indicates some kind of blood relationship). Aunty Joan's stern assessment swam before my eyes and I almost fainted.

As previously stated, Yorkshire people are also short on words and long on actions as my father's sister swept me up and dragged me towards home muttering half comprehended words such as:

'Right my lad; let us see what your ... You ... a doctor ... I can't believe our Arthur would ... condition!'

I did not know my dad's name was Arthur and I felt quite privileged. In those days, adults were only addressed by their surnames unless an intimate relationship existed and then only in private. To my great relief and surprise, I was not in trouble when I was finally dragged, semi-conscious into our kitchen. Mum had suspected my condition and displayed only concern.

Three days later and two weeks before my first secondary school day, I sat forlornly on the settee with a fractured Tarsal bone. A plaster cast adorned my leg up to the knee. Colin, who is 18 months younger than me, had decorated the caste with various drawings and clever statements that made my sister, Judy, giggle when she saw the things he had written on the back. I could not see Colin's epistles, although in retrospect all I needed to do was look in a mirror. Judy refused to divulge them despite my desperate entreaties. My adventuring days had been temporarily halted.

I was terrified that my first day at school would involve limping around in a caste. In two weeks, I would face the ultimate character examination: my first day at Grammar School.

Again, in my little imaginative world, I would defy the odds and walk again. I would suffer indescribable agony like the famous World War II pilot, Group Captain Sir Douglas Bader, who flew Spitfires even after having both legs amputated. My condition was, of course, not serious, but overcoming all odds was fundamental to an eleven-year old psyche

I would dedicate my miraculous recovery to my purpose in life; willing to undertake any pain to achieve the ultimate goal.

5. Not the Expected Holiday Break

In reality, I was ordered to remain off my feet for two weeks under pain of, well, something not repeatable by a pre teenage boy. But, thankfully, my foot healed, the caste was removed and I was able to take my place as a Year 1 innocent at the esteemed and scary Harrogate Grammar School.

6

Secondary School (The Hero in Tears)

Otley Road was a part of town that Dad was familiar with as an artisan and definitely not a resident. He had unwillingly left the fire service and started a handy man business with Uncle Ron. I don't know why he left but I think it had something to do with his outspoken attitude to life.

They would clean windows, build sheds, level a tennis court or even clean chimneys. I had helped him on a few occasions. The occasion that I remember most was when Dad had to replace some tiles in Duchy Road, where the poshest of the posh lived.

The house was huge, and Dad had to build a special extension on his wooden ladder to reach the roof. My job was to hold the ladder steady while Dad worked on the roof, a height of four or so stories, replacing broken tiles. Unfortunately for me, he didn't have enough tiles.

'Son, bring us up a couple of tiles.'

'Yes Dad.'

The job had to be done so I would have to climb this rickety old ladder carrying three slate tiles up to Dad. I decided on three tiles as I wanted to make the journey only once, even though they were very heavy for a pre-teen. I am afraid of heights and still have dreams about falling from mountains, buildings and the like. Sometimes I force myself to creep to the edge of a cliff and experience the fear of falling off. Why? I don't know.

I was terrified but I could not let dad down, so I ascended the ladder clinging on to it for dear life until, after an eternity, I reached the roof.

Luckily, Dad could not see me, but my legs were jelly and my heart beating at twice its normal rate. No occupational health and safety in those days!

I had completely forgotten about this incident and I am sure that Dad just thought of it as another job but in a way, it taught me about overcoming fear. My fear of letting Dad down exceeded my fear of heights. With some trepidation, I had decided to leave my comfort zone and trust to my instinct. A good lesson.

What has all this to do with my secondary school. To be honest, not much, but I wanted to put the story in somewhere and Harrogate Grammar School was in the posh side of town where artisans worked but never resided.

I travelled to school via two buses that transported me from my comfortable existence to a totally new and challenging world.

Harrogate Grammar School is an imposing four-storey grey brick building surrounded by playing fields and incarcerating some 1500 adolescent boys and girls. It is a long way from Bilton, not just in distance, but also in culture.

My first day at secondary school did not go well.

As I got off the bus, hundreds of schoolkids jostled and shouted at each other, seemingly in perfect harmony with their environment. I had never felt so alone. I didn't know anybody except Sheila Whitfield from my primary school and she was a girl.

6. Secondary School (The Hero in Tears)

I stood outside the school gates in my obviously brand-new grammar school uniform with my new and first leather school bag draped behind me. I didn't belong. I had never seen so many children in one place and the formidable building that was to be my new school filled me with terror. The only building more than two storeys in Bilton was the church. This building was four storeys high.

I was swept into the building by a flood of babbling children. Inside was a labyrinth of brown wood and white walled rooms where students battled vainly with Latin, French, English, Arithmetic and the like. The inside of the building was, if anything, more frightening than the exterior.

As I was carried along by the throng of kids, we passed classrooms that had a definite nineteenth century look about them. I had never seen anything like them. The floors of polished wood were sloping with brown integrated front opening desks and hard wood fixed benches. There were slots for pencils and inkwells and space for about thirty students. Huge blackboards designated the teacher's domain. There were other mysterious rooms customised for woodworking, metal-working and an art room.

The senior students had started classes some days earlier and as I passed some of the occupied classrooms, I could see teachers bedecked in black gowns and mortar boards pacing around at the front of the class waiting for a confused student trying to conjugate a Latin verb. At least it sounded like Latin.

The school was vast by my standards and incomprehensible to an 11-year-old brought up in a small farming community. Bilton Endowed looked nothing like this imposing centre of education. It had only three classrooms plus a nursery building.

I had been a big fish in a small pond. Now I was a miniscule insect in a vast ocean.

I dragged myself and my schoolbag in the direction where most of the students were heading. I had never felt so alone.

Hundreds of noisy, excited and confident school children passed me. Some huge fearsome sixth formers even had the beginnings of a beard. In those days, students could stay in sixth form for up to three years in order to qualify for university places

The centre piece of the school was the assembly hall, a vast auditorium replete with grand piano and raised stage. Teachers in full mortar and gown regalia appeared to fly around small, concentrated knots of noisy schoolchildren, their gowns, like crows, fluttering behind.

I was carried along reluctantly with the throng, frozen by panic.

The older boys stood nonchalantly at the back, distancing themselves from the chaos around them. The older schoolgirls clustered around portals and palisades in dignified isolation.

Mixed into this human soup were terrified little first formers, completely disoriented and alone in the crowd. Their brand-new school uniforms and leather school bags that were shown off to Aunts and Uncles, now proclaimed them as raw beginners to be taunted and teased by their superiors.

The begowned and mortared teachers entered the milling crowd like sheepdogs singling out the newbies. The teachers had performed this well practiced art and could identify a newbie from the masses of other students.

We reacted like panicked sheep, fleeing from these wraiths but eventually we were shepherded to the very front of this mass of confusion. I felt very exposed. Behind us were the mass of returning students. In front were the formidable throng of teachers, bedecked in their black regalia.

Once we were in place they did not need to quieten us, we were frozen in panic. A cadre of black suited solemn judges appeared on the stage. These were the head teachers, deputy principal and principal.

I looked around for solace in this alien world, looking for some sign of belonging, but none came. We stood between the stage and the alien student congregation. In front of us were the horsemen of the apocalypse, behind us a gaggle of sniggering seniors.

6. Secondary School (The Hero in Tears)

The headmaster was the last to appear and his entrance was signified by a hush that rippled through the assembly. The gown he wore had a fur lined covering that signified some unknown academic achievement. He strode to the podium, the master of all he surveyed, a godlike creature. All others acknowledged their subservience by their silence.

We were too terrified to comprehend his message. He spoke in the language of the gods, was that Latin, spreading wisdom and insight. The teachers would nod appreciatively. The mass behind us started to shuffle restlessly after fifteen minutes of his missal.

We just wanted to get out.

We craven first formers, still frozen in panic, did not understand this alien ceremony. I felt like a sinner, awaiting judgement.

A small commotion at the front of the returning students discharged a stray newbie. He was in the wrong place, a cardinal sin, and was expelled as an outcast from their presence.

He looked like a panicked sheep lost on the moors. He turned and twisted, looking for escape but none came.

What came was a tall boy, with badges and other insignias of rank; a prefect. Faced with such an apparition, the boy panicked and headed back from where he had been expelled. but the students formed an impenetrable wall and he bounced back into the arms of the waiting prefect. He stood, too terrified to move

And then the prefect smiled. We could not determine whether the smile was one of malice or sympathy but it had the desired effect of calming the unfortunate and he was easily shepherded back into our midst.

The black haired, black browed, black chinned principal frowned momentarily at this sacrilegious interruption and continued his words of wisdom.

The crowd returned to sombre silence. The first form was subsequently ignored as the rest of the school continued with familiar rituals such as the Lord's Prayer, School Hymn and various addresses from the head teachers. We stood uncomprehending as the interminable ceremony dragged on, each minute increasing our nervousness.

At last, the ceremony was over.

I expected a panicked rush to avoid the impending slaughter, but the fearsome posse of teaching staff and prefects restricted us to the confined area at the front of the assembly.

The prefects were even more frightening than the teachers. They were students but they were huge and hairy (well some of the boys had the black stain of a shaved beard.) with a threatening malevolence that said 'Teachers have to obey the rules but we don't - We are the rules and you are our playthings'.

After what seemed an eternity, the Principal and Head Teachers left the stage in the same dignified manner as their entrance. All but the cowering first formers were finally dismissed. They left in a swarm, clattering, banging and shouting as they went to their unknown destinations.

We were left in silence, waiting for the next frightening confrontation. We were an uneasy mob of cattle, exemplified by low murmurings and restless shifting feet, but after some time a lady, who I later discover to be the deputy principal, approached us and smilingly asked for quiet while she announced the class names and the individuals assigned to each class. She was the first friendly face in the ordeal and I will never forget her.

The class rolls were read out starting with the top-rated class, 1A1. The class teachers appeared from hidden corners of the hall and gathered their flock together before shepherding them to their allotted classroom.

I was a good student and expected my name to be read out in the top class but alas this was not to be. Students from the top four classes, 1A1, 1A2, 1B1 and 1B2 were read out. My name was not among them. I had flashbacks to Miss Dickinson's arrangement of students in merit order.

6. Secondary School (The Hero in Tears)

The four lesser classes did not follow the same nomenclature and were named after the first letter of the class teacher's surname, 1G for Mr. Groves, 1H for Mr. Herbert.

There was only one class to go, Mr. Green's class 1G2, the bottom class in the school. I would be unable to face my mother if my name were to be read out. The bottom class! The shame would be unbearable.

I could not go home as a failure. I would just get on a bus, any bus, and get off at its terminus where nobody knew of my abject failure as a grammar school student. In deference to my parents, they never put pressure on me to succeed academically. My fear of failure was, and still is, a demon that I have not yet conquered.

My name was not read out and my disappointment turned to paralysis as I found myself alone in the middle of this enormous amphitheatre. My shame was complete. I was not to be even admitted to the school.

I remembered my proud parents escorting me on one of our infrequent sorties into town to buy my new uniform. How proud they were as I was fitted with a brand new and expensive uniform. My fondest memory is of the school bag. It was real-leather and smelt like heaven.

But back to the story. For the second time in my life, well that's all I will admit to, I broke down in inconsolable tears. It must have been quite a sight after the preceding pomp and ceremony. Through my tears, I could just see the last of Mr. Green's class looking pityingly at me before they disappeared from the hall.

A little kindness and consideration is often dismissed as unimportant, but I will always remember the response of the Deputy Principle to my distress. She shepherded me to her imposing teak lined office, sat me down and with a sympathetic demeanour and soothing rhetoric, extracted the main details of my case, ascertained that my paperwork had been lost, assessed my potential capability, assigned me to the second top class and escorted me to my new classroom. I cannot remember her name, but I will remember her face and words for ever.

7

Whatever Happened to Sheila Whitfield?

Sheila Whitfield remains an anathema. We were never friends as such and I never felt any romantic attachment to her. She never competed with me academically or in sport and the only commonality we had was that we both went to the same primary and secondary school. In fact, she and I were the only first year students that had made it to Harrogate Grammar from our primary school. But she was far more emotionally intelligent than me. She always treated me with respect and concern. I think I missed a trick as she was both attractive and intelligent, but, in my naivety, I was blind to her charms.

She came third in primary school, I was second and teacher's pet and son of the headmaster, Peter Brown was first.

When I was finally ushered into my classroom by the kindly Deputy headmistress, Sheila was there. Her smile of recognition was only the second friendly sign in a morning of turmoil. Perhaps

I was ashamed, (boys don't cry), or I was just overcome with my situation. In any case, I did not return her smile and I will always regret it. Even though she was a girl. We were sort of friends, and for my entire time at Harrogate Grammar School, we were in the same class. Yet for some reason she did not rate on my list of important people which was dominated by Teachers and fellow members of the Colts Rugby XV. My loss!

I do not remember very much about her physical appearance; she had brown curly mid length hair, a medium size nose and slightly protruding lips which enhanced her otherwise unremarkable features. I remember that she had a very engaging smile.

I think that she was very clever (for a girl) and she realised my naiveté and did not press our common background. I found it difficult to start a conversation with her. I really wish that I had got to know her better as we had much in common. I only had time for classes and sport. I readily absorbed Maths, Science, English and the General Studies subjects such as Art and Woodwork but Sheila was much better at French than me. I remember feeling a sense of genuine admiration for her linguistic expertise. In essence, Sheila was an important factor in my adjustment at Grammar School, but I still can't tell you why.

Perhaps I would not have got mixed up with the wrong crowd if I had tried to communicate more effectively with Sheila. The wrong crowd were Peter Radford and his accomplice Peter Newton. I was lonely, a little bit reactionary and susceptible to their flattery and I hung out with these two reprobates. I was only involved in one of their silly schemes, but I will always remember my shame in attempting to 'wag' school. Why I did it, I cannot say. I loved school and looked forward to it every day.

Every school has their 'cools' and the two Peters were the epitome of cool. My response to school was to challenge every moment. I loved lessons and I loved sport, but they intimated that there was more to life, such as challenging authority. I was naive and impressionable, and they led me astray. In retrospect, I was a coiled spring, a wannabe, trying to impress this world of my betters. They gave me a sanctuary, a place where you did not have to worry about school or success. A place where you could just drift down the stream of life.

I was impressed for the wrong reasons. The reasons were smoking in the toilets and various teacher traps such as gluing books together. One of their escapades involved the prettiest girl in the class, June Park, who had developed a slight swelling in her blouse and wore make up. The lads figured that she had started to wear women's stuff like corsets, a stunning and stimulating possibility for three teenage boys. It was decided to place a drawing pin strategically on her seat. The theory was that' if she was wearing the thick corsets of the day, the pin would stick but not penetrate. If she was not wearing corsets then the anticipated yelp of pain would provide some compensation. As it happened, she was wearing corsets and spent the whole day with a round brass drawing pin sticking out of her rear. Oh! the shame!

The two Peters were enterprising but unfortunately not very bright. They planned an escape from school after morning assembly. Truant was considered a serious offence and usually resulted in the administration of the cane on the bottom.

We were to meet in the bicycle sheds and go from there. Where we were going to go was irrelevant to the plan. At 09:15, we duly crept out of our designated classes and assembled in the cycle sheds. Unfortunately, Radford in a double snub to the school, decided to smoke a cigarette that he had stolen from his father. The pungent smell in the confined space brought the Prefects from their gate guarding duties and we were discovered. I still remember the feeling of abject terror and guilt whilst waiting outside the headmaster's office for my sentence. I intend that this will be a 'G' rated book and will omit details of the punishment.

During my second year, I fell in love.

I was besotted by a fellow second former called Gillian Fleming who attended the same school and church as me. I recall sitting at the dining table doing my homework when she came to our house to enlist me in a church fellowship event. She wore the very unflattering grey wool stockings, black shoes and grey tunic dress of a Harrogate Grammar Junior schoolgirl, but I can still see her now as a beautiful vision.

I don't know why or what caused the dramatic reaction that followed. My mouth went dry, I lost the power of speech and could only glance fleetingly at this apparition of beauty when I thought she was not looking.

With due respect to Gillian, I do not think she was particularly sensuous or pretty but at that moment she became my whole world.

The courtship was brief and insignificant, but I can still sense the brush of her lips against mine in our only kiss. It happened outside of the Fish and Chip shop in Kings Road on a warm summer evening.

I recall sitting next to her in church, at a respectful distance of course. Who could have seen the sly glances and coy smiles that passed between us? On one occasion, I was allowed to walk her home. The relationship was never serious enough for me to meet her parents but she told me where she lived and I spent some time standing outside her house, hoping for a glimpse of this teenage paramour.

After a month, the relationship was over when a fourth former, who travelled on the same bus, won her affection by tying her school tie in so many tight knots that she had to beg him to untie them.

She obviously liked strong men. I was cast aside and ignored.

The flame was briefly reignited when my family's emigration to Australia piqued her interest and she agreed to become my girlfriend again. She even allowed me to hold her hand on special occasions, provided no one else was present. Shortly after, we left for Australia and I never saw or heard from her again.

Thinking back, I was in a particularly good place at that time. I was doing well at my studies and had a painting and essay exhibited in the town library. I was a member of the colts first fifteen and played cricket for the school but most of all, I had a girlfriend. I doubt if Gillian would remember me, but I will always remember her.

8
Ten Pound Poms

One-night Dad came home and announced that the family was moving to Australia. Not just the other side of the world but a different universe away. A lot bigger than England, dry, lots of desert, kangaroos, good cricketers, aboriginals. And the capital was Sydney! (We were wrong about quite a few things).

'Hang on there is a P&O passenger ship that was featured in 'The Eagle', (a weekly boy's magazine), called The Canberra. That's right, the capital is Canberra but where that is, is anybody's guess.'

Dad ordered the Reader's Digest World Atlas so that we could look at a map of Australia. We discovered that most people lived on the Eastern Seaboard that the map showed as green indicating good farmland and lots of trees. The map showed the rest of Australia in various shades of brown. It looked pretty sparse and 'deserty' to us. There appeared to be only two main towns in this area, Adelaide and Perth. Dad said he had been to Perth on Rest & Recreation during the war. I thought that they must have schools and things but no woods and very few people.

The Bachelor Gardens Community was not impressed, nor were the family, most of whom lived in Bachelor Gardens, at least on Dad's side. Not only would we travel outside Yorkshire but to the other end of the world. I think some people thought we would fall off the edge. We were going a long way past Cornwall and Devon.

Personally, I was confused and a little dismayed. I would have to give up school and rugby and the chance that Gillian would be my girlfriend again. I didn't hold much hope for the latter, but I loved school and sport.

So, what were the positives?

Australia boasted a cricket team that regularly thrashed England in the Ashes: a positive.

There was also country next to Australia called New Zealand and they had the best Rugby team in the world: a second positive.

Australia also had good weather which suited an outdoor type like me.

I was dubious about the kangaroos in the main street but that did not unduly worry me. I was a farm boy and was used to animals.

Australia was so far away, and travel was so expensive that I thought it would be a long time, if at all, before we returned. In fact, it would be fifteen years before I returned with a wife and two children.

In these days of international travel, it may seem a small thing but in 1964, just like the original convicts, it seemed like a life sentence. The journey would take six weeks plus by sea. A two to three-day airflight was possible for the more economically advantaged but it was way beyond our means.

Nonetheless, at 6:30am on a cold and grey morning (following a dark and stormy night) in April 1964, the family set off for Australia from Harrogate Railway Station. I don't recall any tearful farewells or requests to 'come back soon.' In fact, I think most folk never expected to see us again. The station was almost deserted except for the mandatory porter with brown luggage and a bored expression and our next-door neighbour, Mrs. Cooksey, the only one to acknowledge our departure.

8. Ten Pound Poms

We were bound for Southampton, which was somewhere down south. I remember the thrill of looking out of the train window at vistas previously unknown on my third railway journey. For some reason, Clapham junction, the largest railway junction in England, stands out in my mind. Not the station, but the myriad of connecting and interconnecting railway lines bound for who knows where.

In those days, it took most of the daylight hours to traverse England from North to South and as the day waned to darkness, we embarked on the MV Fairstar for the six-week voyage to Australia. (see cover picture.)

The prospect of a long sea voyage was exciting, but as it turned out, my brother Colin and I spent most of the voyage hanging over the side contributing to the organic contents of the world's oceans. I remember my twelve-year-old brother establishing a very warm relationship with two thirteen-year-old twin girls while I looked on enviously. I also remember my mother's care and concern at my chronic see-sickness, a challenge that I have yet to fully overcome.

She suggested that a game of table tennis might take my mind off the sea and help to overcome my seasickness. We played on the windswept rolling back deck and were probably the only people above deck. Every time the ship rolled; the table would accelerate towards the lower side. It made for an interesting match, but I think my mother's tactic was relatively successful.

9
Where Shall We Go?

We had arrived in Australia not even knowing where we were to settle but finished up in Adelaide because Dad remembered a chap who was related to his sister's husband.

'At least there'll be one person whose name I know.'

It seems strange today, but we emigrated to Australia not knowing any person or where we would end up.

The ship embarked two immigration officials off the coast of Western Australia. Their job was to process the 1900 or so immigrants. The dining hall was cleared, that is all the tables and chairs were moved to the walls and the two immigration officers sat at a single table, located in the centre of the room.

They wore long white socks, short sleeved shirts, pencil thin ties and tight grey short shorts, the almost obligatory uniform for Australian government employees at that time. Each family was ushered in, interrogated, their Australian destination determined, issued with luggage tickets appropriate to their destination and then sent on their way. The parents would attach the ticket to their luggage in the hold.

Dad and Mum sat on the two seats opposite the officials while the three children clustered around them.

I remember little of the conversation but was able to ascertain that our destination had been determined as Brisbane. Dad went down to the hold and attached our purple destination stickers to our two tea chests, but on his way back to our cabin remembered that his brother in law's sister lived in Adelaide. He decided to go back to the dining hall and request that our destination be changed to South Australia. The officials had no objection and our destination was changed to Adelaide which I knew was in South Australia. On such whimsies, major life changing events occur.

We celebrated Mum's 38th birthday sailing across the Australian Bight and landed in Adelaide on the 19th of June 1964.

We found out later that all our worldly goods, two tea chests, had been lost, possibly because of our change in destination. Perhaps there are some emigrants in Brisbane who benefitted from our loss? We arrived in Adelaide therefore with little more than the clothes we wore.

I love Adelaide but the vista that greeted us in 1964 on our bus trip to the hostel, twenty-two kilometres away, resembled a moonscape. Large ships cannot navigate the Port River to reach Adelaide's port, Port Adelaide and consequently, must offload at Outer Harbour on the coast.

The topology between the coast and the city was flat brown marshland with a few scrubby brown plants that seemed to be struggling for survival. The only significant feature in 1964 amidst the sand and salty marshland was the Pioneer Concrete works. I can still recall that sight. It echoes in my mind like a hellish freeze frame, devouring all before it.

Worse was to come, however!

After a forty-minute journey we arrived at Finsbury Hostel, situated just west of the city abattoirs amongst a cluster of heavy industry factories. We entered via a large metal gate, which led to a rutted unkempt concrete roadway. On our right were a number of clustered Nissan huts, to our left a number of factories and warehouses separated from the hostel by a sad corridor of low scrub.

Welcome to your new home!

10
Finsbury Hostel

If my family were to have a shield and associated motto, it would probably be a Yorkshire Terrier with the words 'Never give up' emblazoned on it. Our first few weeks at Finsbury Hostel certainly tested our resolve.

As previously stated, we were left with only the luggage that we carried on the ship, basically a suitcase of clothes and a Rucksack of odds and ends. What money Dad had (I think about the equivalent of $50 in today's terms), was spent on essentials and we were thus penniless and unable to travel or eat outside of the hostel for several weeks.

To say that the conditions of the Hostel was poor, is a gross understatement. The migrants, who were of various nationalities, lived in two or three-room sections of a Nissan hut (four sections per hut). Four huts were arranged in a square surrounding a concrete toilet block. This meant that each toilet block serviced sixteen families of at least 4 members. There were around twenty or so of these combinations on the hostel plus a larger Nissan Hut which served as a mess hall, a previously abandoned weatherboard shed as a community centre and a sparsely grassed football field.

Little maintenance was carried out, the food was almost inedible, and vermin frequented the toilets and eating areas.

To add to this dismal picture, some of the migrants were from extremely poor and underdeveloped communities and their hygiene standards left much to be desired. The toilet blocks were literally indescribable and a relatively clean-living family such as ours would often scour the adjacent toilet blocks in an effort to find one suitable enough for our ablutions. Basically, you only went when you had to and took advantage of hotel and public facilities whenever you could.

Finsbury, by a whisker, was not the worst of the three migrant hostels in South Australia. Gepps Cross Hostel situated on the other side of the abattoirs, some seven kilometres away was in such a poor state, that the inhabitants literally burnt it down in an effort to secure liveable conditions.

The Hostel conditions and the inability to escape from it due to economic circumstances, contributed to tensions, both social and racial. The atmosphere of the hostel, particularly at night, was charged with impending violence. I recall that we were banned from the vicinity of the community hall because there had been a number of incidents involving knives and other weapons. Whether real or assumed, this led to a gloomy menacing atmosphere that disheartened impressionable children.

Recent conversations with my family have suggested that my brother, who was subjected to some bullying and intolerance, was significantly affected by his time at Finsbury, just like another famous inmate, Jimmy Barnes, who was at the hostel at the same time as we were and migrated to Elizabeth as most poms did in those days. Unfortunately for him, Jimmy did not have a supportive family and descended into violence and drug taking before recovering from his experience and becoming an Australian singing icon. Good on him!

10. Finsbury Hostel

I confess that, at the time, I was so caught up in my own life that I did not realise or appreciate the scale of Colin's problem. He would be the last person to make an issue of this but looking back I believe his disposition did change from an outgoing fun kid to a more wary and subdued persona.

I recall one incident that relates to my brother in particular, but more generally illustrates the potential violence that usually lay just under the surface.

My brother came home from school one day with a blooded nose and several other wounds that indicated that he had been 'in a scrap'. He was reluctant to reveal the circumstances that led to his condition, but Mum persisted.

She had heard that a small group of Irish kids had been harrowing young kids, including Colin, my twelve-year-old brother. Eventually he had to confess that he had indeed been waylaid by this gang.

Naturally, this incensed my father who set out to intercept the perpetrators, ordering me to accompany him. I hate fighting but suspected that my role would be to act as the enforcer in this matter as it would not be appropriate for my father to physically attack young teenage children. My suspicions were proved to be correct.

There were not many places to hide in the hostel and we found the gang lurking in the next quadrangle to ours. There were three of them. Their leader, Terry, an Irish boy with a chip on his shoulder, was known to me as a loudmouth and bully. My father challenged the boy, demanding that he confessed to assaulting my brother. The Irish boy replied with such language that if taken seriously would cast doubt not only on my father's parentage but also his claim to humanity.

It was a difficult situation for my father. Clearly, he could not discipline this 13-year-old physically as that would contravene our family's strict moral code.

A stalemate existed until Colin, eager for revenge, approached the gang. The two lackeys immediately attacked him. His baby-faced looks belied a somewhat pugnacious manner and the battle commenced. I had no time to see what was going on as the leader turned to face me. He issued another torrent of abuse as he charged headlong. I will never forget the violence on his face.

Colin was acquitting himself well. He was not exactly winning but he seemed to be able to repulse the two-pronged attack whilst I faced the leader.

Dad had approached the situation expecting an apology from the gang. Their actions confirmed that conciliation was not possible.

'If that's the way you treat adults, then you deserve all you get.' I had no idea as to what they would 'get' but it obviously involved Colin and myself and fisticuffs.

We realised that it was up to my brother and I to defeat the gang. Dad obviously had faith in our fighting capability. He shook his head and turned to return to our hut

He clearly had a confidence in us that I for one, did not feel. As I said, I hated fighting. This was a 'High Noon' situation but thankfully, none of us carried weapons. I was rather perplexed and honestly did not know what to do and for a while just stood there. The two lackeys, disheartened by my father's words and Colin's belligerence, turned and fled leaving myself and Terry remaining on the battlefield.

My opponent, not known for his subtlety or conversation, resolved this stalemate by rushing blindly towards me with raised fists. I was still unsure of what I was supposed to do and pushed him aside causing him to fall over.

Assuming that my role was now completed, I turned to go, only to catch another headlong rush. His strategy was simple.

Years of bottled up frustration was funnelled into a bull like charge designed to trample me into submission. I still remember the look in his eye and the tension on his face.

Unfortunately for him, his charge was completely predictable and, as before, I was able to avoid his onslaught and push him to the ground. The other Terry was still flushed with uncaged hostility and fired off another volley of such invective and profanity that would have caused the coarsest of men to blush just as Dad returned to the quadrangle. I don't know if Colin had asked him to return or if Dad was not as confident in my prowess as he had made out

The red veil of violence was in my opponent's eyes and was ready to bludgeon any opposition, regardless of size or capability.

I recall looking at this ball of angst and feeling sorry for him. I stood my ground awaiting his next move. Perhaps he had had enough, after all he must have realised that I was stronger than him. I was not really concerned about my own safety. I was fit and a keen rugby player and quite competent to deal with anything he could throw at me.

Again, the assault came without subtly or science. He merely charged at me again. It took little skill on my part to avoid the charge and he stumbled past me and fell to the ground.

Game over!

No! Nothing could assuage his wrath. I remember thinking that his rage was not really aimed at me but at the world which had undoubtedly dealt him a poor hand.

I tried to pacify him, but my words were unheeded as he turned and charged at me for the umpteenth time. I felt like a reluctant Toreador, moving aside as the bull charged. Again, he passed me and stumbled but this time he retained his feet.

I looked at him, my eyes pleading with him to stop.

Again, and again he charged and again I pushed him aside until he eventually managed to strike a glancing blow on my shoulder with his elbow. The blow did not hurt. He was too exhausted to land a telling blow, but it did force me out of my torpor, and I met his next charge with my fist. The speed and recklessness of his charge resulted in a fairly significant though unintended blow to his chin and he collapsed at my feet. I presumed that this would end the matter, but I underestimated his defiance and he attacked again, to be met again by my fist to the side of his head. I wish to say at this point that I was not punching the unfortunate lad, he merely ran into my fist.

To cut a long story short, this cycle was repeated many times until he eventually fell exhausted to the ground. I had never experienced such violence before or since and I felt sorry for his condition. The next day, I saw him in the mess hall with bruises and cuts covering his face; wounds that I had inadvertently inflicted. I remember that incident with some regret, as I allowed events to develop rather than taking control.

We ate in the mess hall and to be fair the authorities were not entirely to be blamed for the decrepit state of the place. As previously stated, a small number of the hostel inhabitants, I could not call them residents, had very primitive habits. Spilled food covered the floor, chairs and tables and a significant cleaning effort was required before sitting down.

My family's lifestyle was simple but relatively hygienic and consideration for others was a hallmark of our culture. We found the experience of eating in mess hall unpleasant and to be avoided whenever possible. In fact, if the mess hall proved to be in an unacceptable state, we would often return to our hut to eat. This meant returning to the hall to wash our utensils as there were no washing facilities in our quarters but it was preferable to sitting in the squalor of the so called 'dining hall'.

The food was provided by a mass catering company called Nationwide at a minimal cost. I believe that the government who funded the hostels provided a ridiculously small amount of money which was further reduced by the profit made by the catering company. I remember black meat that could not be cut and had to be chewed into submission, soggy chips and a mess of unrecognisable vegetables For the first few weeks, we literally had no money and were obliged to eat at the government's miniscule expense in the aptly named, 'mess hell'.

Dad worked as a fitter in a factory, a carpenter building outback schools and a couple of other entirely forgettable jobs because he was too old to resume his career as a Fireman. It is a great credit to him and my mother that he was able to work at several low paying jobs and still save enough money to pay for the deposit on a house in just over six months. His positive attitude was not reflected by all of the inhabitants, some of whom spent two or more years in the hostel, working intermittently or not at all, waiting for the opportunity to return home.

It has been estimated that over a quarter of the inmates returned to their place of origin without ever experiencing real Australian conditions. Even though it was of their own making, they must have had a poor view of Australia. Whingeing poms perhaps, but with some justification.

There is not much else to tell of the hostel. I attended Woodville High School, which educated a fair percentage of Finsbury immigrants. The school was not overly flushed with funds, but the classrooms were reasonable. We played cricket and soccer with a tennis ball, much as I had done at Harrogate Grammar School, on a small asphalt quadrangle separated from the girl's area by a high wire fence.

I recall that the duty teachers were instructed not to allow the boys near the fence to prevent any unacceptable behaviour although I do not know what we could have done being separated by a ten-foot-high barrier.

My time there was fairly uneventful; I was very studious and did not make any real friends. One noteworthy academic achievement was my second placing in the year for Australian History, beaten, as it happens by another migrant, from Scotland.

I was also keen on Sport and played soccer for the Under 16 hostel team. The hostel's meagre maintenance budget did not stretch to sprinklers or grass cutting machinery, so the oval had become a clay pan where the occasional tuft of scrubby grass struggled to the surface. The goalposts had been fashioned from water pipes painted white. No sissy padding for us. The Saturday morning game was a welcome diversion from the rigours of hostel life and I thoroughly enjoyed playing against the other junior teams from the district. Soccer was considered a European game. The other teams had names such as 'Yugal', 'Polonia White and Polonia Blue', 'Croatia' and the like. Interestingly enough, we were wary of the Europeans on the hostel but had no such fears on the soccer field.

After six months, Dad had saved enough money to put a deposit on a house and the family moved up the North Road some twenty kilometres to Elizabeth.

I suppose people are attracted to others of their culture when faced with a strange environment and we were no exception. In any case, we were glad to see the back of the hostel.

11
A Town Called Elizabeth

As soon as my father amassed enough money to pay for a deposit on a house, we moved to 'Pommy Central', the town of Elizabeth, which was almost entirely populated by English families. The Town Planners were not particularly imaginative and the original four suburbs were named Elizabeth North South, East and West. When they ran out of names, they decided to name suburbs after their appearance and Elizabeth Fields came into being.

The suburb was characterised by graded (not sealed) red clay roads, redbrick three bedroom 'project' homes, brown grass, and no trees, but it was home for a year. Dad was employed by the government as a carpenter and spent some time away from home, helping to build rural schools in locations that were isolated from isolated locations. He had no formal training but was the only carpenter building outback schools as far away as Wilpena pound in north eastern South Australia. He was away from home for up to six weeks at a time.

It was a tough time for my mother, attempting to bring up three kids by herself in what could be a hostile environment.

Elizabeth Fields was the cheapest of the suburbs and attracted people who could not afford to live elsewhere. A number of these families were dysfunctional, a polite way of saying violent[7], and were completely consumed by their own troubles. My mother found Elizabeth Fields less than friendly and was unable to make many friends. I remember our next-door neighbour was an ex-boxer with an alcohol problem. He was ok when sober but after a few drinks, he became a blubbering mess and threatened self-harm. On several occasions, Mum would have to supervise my brother and I to put him to bed. Mum is a very caring soul and was greatly saddened by these experiences.

Elizabeth was not a safe place in those days. There were areas that you did not go to, gangs roamed the streets looking for trouble and drugs were not uncommon. It always seemed to me that the anxiety and sense of dread that permeated the hostel had been transferred to Elizabeth. I suppose it was not surprising, as many of the families from the hostel migrated to Elizabeth.

My brother Colin always seemed to be able to attract girls whereas I was still terrified by them. I was relatively happy at Elizabeth High School even though I didn't have a girlfriend. Judy carried on with her normal unflustered demeanour.

One bright spot on the 'girl front' occurred when I was invited to a party by Colin. He had organised a party where I met a girl, Willa, that I rather liked but I was not sure if the feeling was mutual. I was too shy to follow it up and the opportunity was lost. Nevertheless, I was relatively content so naturally it was time for a change. Again!

Dad had always joked that, although he knew that the three of us were his offspring, he had become concerned when he discovered that we had the same milkman as in Bilton. This is a disservice to my mother, who endured Dad's wanderlust from Yorkshire to Finsbury

---

7. Jimmy Barnes in his excellent book, *Working Class Man*, describes both hostel living and the gang mentality of Elizabeth in those days.

Hostel to Elizabeth and subsequently to Woomera without complaint. As it transpired, something must have happened during one of Dad's infrequent visits, as Mum announced the impending arrival of a fourth sibling. Raymond, who was born on the 10th December 1965.

I completed my scouting career in the same manner that it had started: lost, and soaked to the bone. I also had a 'Gillian Fleming' experience. A girl guide who I did not know, visited my home to invite me to a scout/guide's social function. She entered the house whilst I was doing my homework and I fell in love. (again) I cannot remember her name, but she had red hair and an engaging smile. A week later, my heart was broken yet again, when the eighteen-year-old senior scout leader cut in whilst we were dancing at a social event and my amorous prospects returned to 'negligible'. Jan, the scout leader, was later to 'out' himself as a person who preferred non platonic relationships with men and ended up in some trouble for his extracurricular activities with younger boys: Served him right!

Even though rain is infrequent in South Australia, wet seemed to characterise my time in the scouts. The next 'wet' occurred at the Easter Venture, a four-day hike for senior scouts (fifteen to seventeen years old). We had arrived at our campground at the Barossa Reservoir in the pouring rain. Scouts were supposed to select their camp sites with due regard to the environment, but the obstacles caused by the rain had slowed all of the participants and most of us arrived exhausted in pitch black conditions. The only flat ground available turned out to be on the banks of the dam overflow.

The rain continued unabated and around midnight the whole campsite was inundated with half a metre of water. The only shelter available was the Besser blocked toilet facility in which sixty bedraggled young lads sought shelter. We were crammed in like sardines and there was no room to sit but at least the body heat increased the temperature slightly. I recall drinking pea and ham soup, pressing against the mass of bodies in order to avoid further dampening in the urinal.

Elizabeth High School played Rugby as all English biased schools should do. I was lucky to be selected for the under 16 South Australian Rugby Team that travelled to Perth in 1965 for the Australian Rugby Championships. We were not terribly successful, winning only one game; against Tasmania but we were competitive and got within twenty points of the NSW and Queensland teams.

We were billeted with players from the Western Australian Teams. My billet was notable because my host, Tim, who played for the Western Australia second team, had an incredibly attractive twin sister called Penny. We enjoyed each other's company but there was an obstacle to expanding the relationship. She had a boyfriend, Geoffrey (not Jeffrey) who played on the wing for the West Australian First XV and was the Junior WA hurdles champion.

I did not like Geoffrey with a 'G' and the feeling was mutual. He was a private schoolboy of the worst kind; overconfident and arrogant. I was expected to bow to his superiority; his Steerforth to my David Copperfield. I suppose my working-class background showed because he rarely deigned to acknowledge my presence.

The big day arrived when we were to play Western Australia at Perry Lakes Stadium where the Commonwealth Games had been held a few years earlier. I did not have my best game. At one point, I dived over the line to score a try before being engulfed by the opposition forward pack, only to discover that the line was in fact five yards further on.

As scrum half, my job in defence was to cover the back in case any player broke the line. We were losing by a point or two when high stepping hurdling super athlete Geoffrey broke away and raced down the sideline. I was known for my defence and lined him up for what was to be a try saving tackle.

I launched myself with all the determination I could muster to bring him down to the turf only to find myself grasping at thin air. I crashed to the ground to see Geoffrey with a 'G' look back with disdain as he crossed the try line. But pride comes before a fall and Geoffrey was so distracted by his triumph that he crossed both the try line and the back line and almost collided with the back fence. Geoffrey with a 'G' was out and dirty kneed urchin boy was in.

A few years later, I met Penny in Perth during my Naval Training Cruise. She was a trainee Nurse and very affable. We had a very pleasant time, but the magic had gone, and we never saw each other again.

Back in Elizabeth, things were going relatively well. I was doing well at school and sport and had even made a couple of friends. As they say in the movies, 'I could have had it all'.

Dad's first love, after my mother, was the Fire Service and he had applied several times for a position with the South Australian Fire Brigade but, at thirty-nine, he was considered too old. He kept trying though and eventually landed a job, not with the SA Brigade, but with the Commonwealth Government at a place called Woomera, 600 kilometres north of Adelaide. My brother, Raymond, was born, six weeks before our next migration.

In early January 1966, the family embarked on another adventure aboard an old piston engine Douglas Dakota. I mention the plane because the journey was rough, and, as with any erratic motion I became chronically motion sick.

I recall sitting on the car park curb at Woomera Airfield with my mother as we both attempted to overcome the nausea in sweltering heat. The irony was lost on me but in two years, we had come from the frozen north of England to the sweltering heat of Australia's hinterland. Welcome to the desert.

12

To the Desert

The North of South Australia is dominated by thousands of kilometres of gibber plain, saltbush and the occasional cluster of sand dunes. It is vast and joins up to the Nullarbor plain to complete one of the most desolate areas in the world. And yet it has life. The indigenous people have inhabited this area for thousands of years, subsisting on a diet of lizards and the occasional desert vegetable. To be honest, it is a weird place for a family steeped in the culture and climate of North Yorkshire to settle. Surprisingly, the Parker family loved it.

It is difficult to describe the transition of the Parker family from working class North Yorkshire to the desert of Northern South Australia, but it speaks to the adaptability of human culture. It is perhaps appropriate to attempt to describe the environment that we were thrown into.

Pimba stands approximately 5 kilometres from the township of Woomera. It owes its existence to the transcontinental railway and was built in the late 1940s as a railway 'fettlers' settlement (fettle means to 'make good, maintain'). It is the 'gateway to Woomera'; a symbol of outback life contrasting with the high-tech intrusion of the rocket range on its doorstep. Nowadays, Pimba is a tourist attraction, 190 kilometres north of Port Augusta and a major stop on the tarmac road to Alice Springs.

At 'the ponds', a sandy oasis on the outskirts of Woomera, a solitary headstone stands guard over an 8-metre square area of white sand. It marks the death of a young stockman in 1893 who fell off his horse, broke his leg and crawled several kilometres looking for shade and water before dying a lonely death. Ironically, the water that could have saved his life was a mere six inches below the dried-up pond.

100 kilometres away, across a single lane rutted car killer of a track, is Andamooka, on the southernmost vein of Australia's vast opal fields. Andamooka is the forgotten opal town. It is too far from anywhere to be a tourist town like Cooper Pedy and it's a dead end. There is nowhere else to go. The road, such as it is, terminates at the opal fields, surrounded by a few remaining cave-like humpies where old time miners still dig. The single store is a ramshackle shapeless building, half buried in the desert sand and regularly features specials on methylated spirits.

80 kilometres southeast of Pimba, in the middle of a vast gibber plain is Roxby Downs Station. Roxby was settled in the 1890s and boasts a ramshackle shearing shed and a few outhouses that serve as accommodation for the shearers during the mad flurry of shearing month. Most of the time it stands abandoned, surveying the vast featureless gibber in the unlikely hope that creatures other than the big reds, granddaddy emus and six-foot racing goannas, will look for shelter in its windswept, sun caked solitude. Of course, we were completely ignorant of this when we moved to Woomera but now, I feel a connection to that unforgiving wasteland.

Woomera's history began in 1947, over twelve thousand miles away in grey, rain swept, post war England where a meeting of scientists and senior public servants selected Woomera as the Long-

12. To the Desert

Range Weapons Research Establishment. They made a 'strategic' cold war decision to build a weapons testing facility in Australia. It is improbable that they were aware of the impact that their decision would have, halfway round the world in an area populated only by a few kangaroos and an occasional aboriginal family passing through on their nomadic travels.

Woomera was born as a row of Nissen huts, transported from Adelaide, and occupied by UK and Australian servicemen, surveyors and a couple of hardy scientists. The first rocket, an early version of the British, 'Thunderbird' ground to air missile, was launched from Woomera in March 1949, six months before a second momentous event, my birth, took place.

On 15th January 1966, when the Parker family moved to Woomera, it was a thriving service orientated village of around 5,000 people.

My father, a Fireman first and last, was in his element. Fortunately, most qualified Fireman were not prepared to move to the isolation of the Australian desert, so Dad was welcomed with open arms to the Commonwealth Fire Service in Woomera, appropriately as a Senior Fireman. Mum, red haired and adverse to heat and the Sun was not so well adjusted but, as always, she never complained.

We flew to Woomera on an old Piston engine Douglas DC3 that struggled like a wounded bat in a hurricane to climb the 6,000 feet to its cruising altitude. The day was boiling and the DC3 had only ineffective air blowers. Salt Lake thermals would violently and randomly toss the fragile old plane up, down, sideways and at one point almost upside down (or at least that is how it seemed to a 16-year-old, vulnerable to motion sickness). Up like a demonic lift, down in free fall for thousands of feet (well maybe hundreds)

My brother, Raymond, was six weeks old, ensconced in a swinging baby hammock and completely oblivious to the pain suffered by his eldest brother.

I have never been a good traveller and I spent my first thirty minutes in Woomera sitting on a kerb divesting myself of the entire contents of my stomach, oblivious to the 117-degree temperature.

We had arrived in Woomera on the hottest day on record.

Woomera was a Services town like no other. Access was so restricted that a visitor could only enter Woomera after a thorough security investigation and authorisation process which took several months. The occasional tourist or friend of a resident who attempted access by turning up at 'Pimba' gate would be politely instructed to return to their point of origin.

This isolation and consequent subculture of independence and exclusivity was not unlike the atmosphere of my early days in Yorkshire. Both environments were special and unique, if insular.

This book was designed to be a recollection of events in my life and not subject to personal perspectives. However, it seems to me that the thrill of living in so many different environments suggests that focussed caring communities are the best environments for families. I consider myself to be fortunate to have so many different experiences and to be honest, Woomera was the pinnacle of my adolescence

13

Woomera

My father had progressed to Assistant Chief Fire Officer and prided himself on always being the first to respond to the World War II air raid siren which warned everybody within 100 kilometres that somewhere a fire was burning. Dad was an ex-Royal Marine and everything had to be organised and in order so when the alarm sounded, regardless of the time, he was always first to the Fire station.

I, as senior offspring, would stand at the back door with his fire axe and belt, Colin, the second born, with his helmet and Judy, the second youngest, with the boots. Other clothing was optional and Dad would often rush past in his pyjamas, snatching the fireman's essentials with Mum in hot pursuit with his trousers. Once I even drove our station wagon onto the soccer pitch, mid game, not stopping as Dad launched himself into the rear of the wagon. Colin with helmet was in the backseat accompanied by our boots carrying sister. It wasn't until after the emergency that Dad remembered that although I had had a few lessons, I did not have a licence. The boots, incidentally, were later rendered unusable after a magnesium fire in a rocket maintenance area literally melted them to Dad's feet. This pleased my sister enormously.

The main vegetation in the Woomera area was saltbush, bluey brown desert plants usually no more than 18 inches high, and the occasional Mallee scrub. On one occasion, a brush fire was ignited after an unsuccessful rocket firing started a fire at Commonwealth Hill, at that time the largest sheep station in the world. The fire raged on a 100-kilometre front and could not be contained, threatening the area's sheep population and worrying Woomera residents. Luckily, it burned itself out in an area of sand hills.

Dad had been monitoring the fire from a helicopter and was puzzled that the fire could spread at all. Saltbush is poor fuel at the best of times and the 10-20 feet between plants made it difficult for one plant to fire another. So how did it spread???

The firemen had a theory and in order to test it, drilled several large but shallow holes in the fire area and discovered that the intertwined root systems were still burning and were responsible for conducting the fire from plant to plant.

A small community of single men worked on the rocket range, which was located beside Lake Koolymilka, 40 kilometres from Woomera village. I considered it a pretty depressing place, as the men appeared to have no outlet for any after work interests except drinking alcohol.

But one should never underestimate human ingenuity and the men had put much of their afterhours energy into building several sailing skiffs and converting their mess into a yacht club. The Salt Lake rarely had water in it but after or sometimes during a major downpour, an impromptu regatta would be held. Personnel would come from all over the range and beyond to attend the famous Koolymilka Regatta.

As in Yorkshire, topics of conversation were usually focussed on the local sports or clubs and the state of the countryside or more particularly, The Port Road.

13. Woomera

In Woomera, the only road out of the village was a 190 kilometre dirt track infamous for its varied and challenging conditions. It was known as 'The Port Road', as it terminated at Port Augusta. Rain could cut the route in a matter of hours, or dust storms and high winds could cover the road in two metres of sand or expose jagged stones capable of ripping tyres to shreds.

The equivalent on the Yorkshire moors were blizzards and heavy snowstorms that on one occasion my father tells me, resulted in a fire engine being lost for several weeks. I don't vouch for the veracity of this statement.

In December 1967, just before I joined the Royal Australian Navy, I was scheduled to drive my family, minus my father, to Adelaide towing an old-fashioned plywood caravan. I had just turned eighteen and had no experience in towing and so decided to master the art by driving around the dirt roads that surrounded Woomera. It is important to note that the only sealed roads in Woomera were in the town or to the rocket range so most of the outlying roads were dirt, occasionally graded to level out most of the holes. Typically, these roads had been graded so many times that the road itself was anything up to a metre below the surrounding countryside. This resulted in a significant bank of dirt, called 'berms', on each side of the road.

I had been driving for some time and was rather pleased with my ability to tow the caravan when I reached the crest of a hill and careered down the other side at a most uncomfortable pace. I panicked somewhat and applied the brakes with too much force which caused the car to swerve and the caravan to sway uncontrollably. Somehow, I managed to avoid overturning but finished up with the caravan 'jack-knifed' over the car towbar with the front wheels overhanging the berm.

I was 40 kilometres from Woomera on a little used dirt road. There were no mobile phones in those days and the likelihood of help arriving was small. I was not worried about my safety but I was terrified of my father's reaction to my inability to extricate myself from a crisis.

Luckily, through a combination of jacking the car up and releasing some air from the tyres, I was able to manoeuvre the car from underneath the caravan and return flustered but unimpaired to Woomera.

This experience stood me in good stead as, when I finally drove the car and caravan down the Port Road, I was able to manage the significant challenges and arrive unscathed at Port Augusta. In this case, the major hazard was the deep ruts caused by the heavy 'Road Trains' that were deeper than my tyres. This resulted in the car and caravan combination sliding on their undersides along the space between the ruts regardless of the action of the brakes or steering. As long as the ruts followed the road there was no danger but it was an unnerving experience.

Woomera's three grass footy fields were kept in pristine condition by recycled water from the sewerage works. Recycled water had in fact turned Woomera into an oasis in the desert. Trees and bushes were planted along the roads and carefully nurtured and watered. Circular earth dams, usually about 3 feet in diameter were built around each plant to retain water, A clay sewerage pipe of two feet in depth was drilled vertically into the soil near the plant and the pipe was crowned with a Billy lid which could be removed so that water could be poured into the pipe and then replaced to limit evaporation.

One drawback of the recycling system was that tomato seeds, despite the best efforts of the water engineers could not be filtered out. As a result, Tomato plants would spring up in lawns, in gutters and even in cracks in the tarmac. Unfortunately, the weather was usually too hot for the plants to mature and bear fruit.

Football was big in Woomera and I learnt how to play Aussie Rules, winning the best and fairest award for my club in my first year. It was a fairly lucrative business. Woomera was full of single men with only alcohol to spend their money on or the occasional weekend foray to Adelaide. Each Saturday after the game, money was collected and distributed to the six best players as adjudged by the Mess.

13. Woomera

I played for the 'Centrals Club', resplendent in Essendon's colours and associated with the Junior Mess where most of the single men belonged. Centrals did not have the panache or style of the Village Club which boasted the support of the Senior Staff Mess, but after a successful game, I often received anything from $5 to $30 dollars for my efforts. In the sixties, just after decimalisation, that was a lot of money.

There were two dirt ovals, McCallum and Woomera West. A grader would be used to clear the gibber stones each week, the oval marked and the game commence. Aussie rules wasn't so bad, if you were quick you could get rid of the ball before being tackled but I received many a bloodied knee playing Rugby League. My brother even played Rugby League for South Australia as the three Woomera teams were the only Rugby League teams in South Australia.

I completed my matriculation at Woomera. The standard was not good even though the teachers tried hard and only two of the fifteen in the matriculation class passed the matriculation exams.

I have many happy memories of my school days in Woomera. In my second year, I was elected by the students as Head Prefect. The election system could be described as proportionally democratic. The Senior Year, each had eight votes, fourth year (penultimate) six votes, third year five and so on down to the primary school. The votes were amassed and the six boys and six girls with the most votes were elected as prefects.

Jenny Malone, the Girl Head Prefect, and I were given quite a deal of responsibility. We would stand in for teachers unexpectedly called away, supervise the primary school playground and organise the social and sporting events on the school calendar. We were even allowed to design our own prefects blazer pocket, which naturally incorporated a rocket taking off in the desert.

The school play was one of the highlights of the year and took place in the very well-appointed Woomera theatre. In 1967, we took on the ambitious project of staging Shakespeare's 'King Lear' which we managed inadvertently to turn from a tragedy to a comedy. Rehearsals had gone very well under the supervision of Miss Schubert, the Head English Teacher, and despite the sheer magnitude of the task, we had reached Act 3 on the night with no real problems.

Buoyed with confidence, we embarked on Act 4, which commenced with a swordfight between the 'goodie' Edgar, and the 'baddie' Edmund ('The wheel has come full circle, I am here'). The two protagonists, Martin and Phil, were two of the more energetic lads in the school and took to the fight with gusto. They became so engrossed in their battle that they continued for several minutes, forgetting that I, as King Lear, was waiting in the wings for my entrance, carrying my dead daughter, the much-wronged Cordelia. When Edmund, the baddie, finally succumbed, I had been holding Cordelia, a very pretty but slightly rotund young lady, for several minutes. King Lear is in a bad way at this stage and is near to death himself but I was not play acting as I stumbled onto the stage with Cordelia in my arms. It was all I could do to utter the immortal lines 'Dead, dead, she is dead' or something resembling that, before dropping Cordelia on the floor from quite a height.

She was a trooper however and instead of vocalising her obvious pain exhaled an elongated grunt which I think the audience interpreted as Post Mortality Syndrome (PMS). I knelt to the ground beside her to utter my final words ' dead, dead, she is finally dead' before collapsing elegantly by her side in the final death scene.

Except that, overcome by the occasion, and in true Shakespearean fashion, I raised myself up to signal my death to the gods before falling full length across the poor unfortunate Cordelia, whose long painful moan was taken by the audience as something more than PMS. Cordelia's final ignominy came as the curtain fell across her neck exposing only her head to the audience. One of the stagehands unceremoniously grabbed her by the feet to pull her back behind the curtain. I can never apologise enough to that poor victim of my heightened dramatic thespianism.

I received my just desserts on the sporting field later that year.

13. Woomera

My younger brother, Colin, and I played on different sporting teams and were quite competitive; well Colin was. As we neared the end of a game between our two clubs, Centrals and Works, my team was behind by five points or just less than a goal. I found myself running into an open goalmouth. I should have put my foot to the ball immediately and our victory would have been assured, but I wanted to savour the moment, and stopped to line up the kick with great care and aplomb. Or so I thought. As I prepared for the final moment, a shadow appeared behind me and I remember little else.

I discovered afterwards that my brother had run some twenty metres from his position and, fuelled by years of being the younger brother, had launched himself into the air and fallen on me from behind, as we would say, 'like a ton of bricks'.

I had wanted to make a good impression but the only impression I made that day, was on the grass.

M.V. Fairstar

Arrival in Australia

13. Woomera

Finsbury Hostel 1960s

Easter Venture

A Douglas Dakota (DC3)

ELDO Launch Site at Lake Hart with Missile Testing Range 'E' in the background

13. Woomera

WRESAT

Woomera Prefects

The Car and Caravan Combination

Cadet 02980

13. Woomera

Royal Australian Naval College 1st XV 1968

Mess Undress (you should see mess dress?)
I am the one on the right

14

From Desert to the Sea

The third aircraft flight of my life was from Adelaide to Sydney to join the Royal Australian Navy. I had no idea what was in store for me, but I would be paid to attend university and this seemed a better option than working my way through a medical degree at Adelaide University.

I did not even know where the Royal Australian Naval College was located. Sydney was the biggest city in Australia so it should be there. On the flight from Adelaide to Sydney, I met John Dikkenberg who was the other recruit from South Australia.

He didn't seem to know where the Naval College was or, at least, he was not prepared to tell me. In today's technology, you would 'google it or 'tweet' one of your friends. The current generation would find it strange but in 1968 there was no internet and no mobile phones and no way to locate it.

Somehow, I do not remember how, we arrived at Sydney Airport and found a bus to the Central Railway station.

Our orders were to report to the RTO (Rail Transport Office) at 2pm and so we did although our onward journey had nothing to do with the railway. I don't know what the inside of the RTO looks like because when we arrived outside it, we were met by an officious looking Naval person, dressed in all whites with a Naval Officer's cap on his crew cut head. It was not a meeting of equals. There was no hello or welcome to the Navy, just a perfunctory, 'Wait here until instructed otherwise'.

The white uniformed Naval person then left us to round up other strays who were not clever enough to determine where the 'RTO' was. We waited for an interminable period, probably thirty minutes, until the white uniformed Naval Person returned with the last of the strays. So, there we were, twenty confused teenagers at the RTO, an officious looking youth in Naval Uniform, and a blue Naval Bus.

The Naval Uniform barked an incomprehensible order. We didn't need interpretation as it was obvious that he wanted us to get on the bus. Like confused sheep at a Sheep dip, we were shepherded one by one into the bus whilst the Uniform continued to bark unnecessary orders. I hadn't expected a 'Welcome to the Navy' indoctrination video but I was totally confused by the lack of information. It seemed, as it would prove to be later, that we were merely military numbers to obey without question. We obeyed.

We found out later that the white uniformed Naval Person was the Chief Cadet Captain, John Lord. Lord by name, Lord by nature.

So, we were on our way to The Royal Australian Naval College. The sooner the better I thought as the bus was smelly and the seats not built for comfort. The Uniform stood at the front of the bus, whilst we were transported to Where? A braver than normal recruit, me, asked 'How far is the Naval College?'

I expected some response, but none came. The Uniform did not respond.

We arrived at our destination which was not the Naval College but a warehouse, The Royal Edward Victualling Yard (REVY) in Darling Harbour, Pyrmont. Why were we there? Only the Uniform knew, and he wasn't about to converse with lower ranks. We piled out of the bus to be confronted with a typical five-story marine warehouse.

The building confronting us was' in some ways like a four-story dolls house. There were no walls on our side of the building, just a platform lift and an inordinate number of open floors. We were confused; why were we there? The uniform had enlisted the help of a number of blue suited sailors who doled out our lunch. Lunch consisted of the most indigestible meat sandwich ever created. The slices of bread were centimetres thick and contained a brown lettuce leaf, and a large slice of leathery meat, complete with half an inch of fat; our first introduction to Naval cuisine.

Again, we were shepherded into a line in order to receive our Naval clothing.

'Parker T. Two pairs of number nine boots. Sign here.'

And so, we progressed through line after line to receive our summer mess undress, our winter mess undress, our summer mess dress (ice cream suits), one sowing kit (naval blue), and so on.

Yes, a sewing kit. Naval Officers may be a privileged community, but they had to learn to sew and to look after their own uniforms.

What did it all mean? We had no idea, but we placed our new uniforms in our newly supplied Naval Chests and waited for somebody to tell us what to do.

After another incomprehensible tirade from the guy in uniform, the Chief Cadet Captain (CCC)[8], we were once more herded on to a bus for the journey to the RANC. The RANC, HMAS Creswell instead of being just down the road, as I had thought, was actually 250 kilometres to the south in Jervis Bay.

As previously stated I am not a good traveller and the three and a half hour trip around the south coast of New South Wales severely tested my intestinal fortitude, but with the discrete use of the paper bag in which the so called sandwich had been served, I was able to cover up my discomfort.

---

8. Everything in the Navy was accompanied by an abbreviation

I won't bore you with my experiences for the rest of the day except to say that we were barked at several more times, formed into a ragged line and subjected to an extended welcoming speech by the College Master of Studies (MOS) and the Naval Captain of the College (CAPT), none of which I can remember.

We were marched around the oval and shown around what was to be our home for the next eighteen months and served with an entirely forgettable meal. At the end of the day, we were assigned our 'cabins', four to a room, complete with metal bunks and a tallboy (cupboard), the only furniture in the cabin.

At 9pm, the lights went out and we were left to consider an unknown future in the darkness to contemplate the error of our decision to join the Navy.

15
Naval College

Jervis Bay Naval College is one of the most beautiful locations in Australia. The college itself, an ex-holiday resort built in 1911, consists of two whitewashed wooden two-storey buildings which accommodated the cadets, joined by a single-storey mess hall. In front of the college is the college oval, known as the quarterdeck, a prohibited place where only the senior cadets were allowed to saunter across to the modern (in 1968) study block opposite. More of that later.

The college area juts out into a picture postcard bay with rolling waves and bleached white sandy beaches. The coastline is pristine with little evidence of human habitation, but to a junior cadet midshipman (CMID) in his first few weeks, it could be and usually was, a place of agony and torment.

In my time, the college was run by the senior cadets with little involvement of the instructors or officers. The archaic discipline had changed little from Nelson's day. At least we couldn't be keelhauled or flogged but minor lapse of concentration could result in extra drill or even worse, 'Number 9s'. Everything from uniforms to punishment had a number.

The day started and ended with the threat of punishment and humiliation. The unstated but obvious objective was to breakdown individualistic or independent characteristics to evoke blind obedience to orders regardless of personal cost. It required tenacity, strength of character and a little bit of cunning to survive unscathed. There were two entry levels. Year 10, the Junior entry and those who had finished Year 12, the Senior Entry.

The Senior Entry were despised by other cadets who had been at the college for two years. Real Naval officers joined at 14 and were immersed in the law of the sea. Senior Entry Cadets were an anathema and not really considered as the real stuff.

To compensate for this, Senior Entry Cadets were required to start as fourth-class cadets, the lowest level. Certainly, they progressed quickly from fourth class to third class before joining their junior entry peers in second class but there was six months of biased discrimination that could be inflicted before the Senior Entry gained their rightful status.

We were at the mercy of the third class, boys still of school age, who controlled our lives and were entitled to mete out certain punishments if we did not obey their sometimes-humiliating demands.

A fourth-class day commenced and ended with discipline.

At 05:30am, a bosun's pipe signalled the start of the day. Bathers and sandshoes were donned for the first exercise of the day, an energetic swim in Jervis Bay, regardless of the weather. Third class cadets would be on hand to ensure that any malingerers were harangued into action. At 06:30, The fourth class assembled in the accommodation stairwell for a particularly nasty little game called 'quick shifts'.

As previously mentioned, there were a multitude of various uniforms for a Naval Cadet, twenty-six of them to be specific, each designated by a number. The Senior Cadets would call a number from the top of the stairs and the hapless junior cadets would be obliged to rush to their cabins, undress from their working dress, ensuring that each article of clothing was folded and stowed as per Naval Standards before donning the requisite uniform and reporting back to the stairwell. Laggards were typically punished with the requirement to run around the outside of the oval for the duration of the morning and or afternoon tea break thus ensuring they received no break or tea.

Quick shifts would continue for about thirty minutes or until the senior cadets tired of the sport. Occasionally, a senior cadet would descend with a ruler to the junior cadets' cabins during the game (to them) and measure the stowed clothing to ensure it complied with regulations. For example, a shirt had to be folded in a specific fashion with a minimum of four buttons, including the top button, buttoned and measuring exactly 8 inches by 12 inches.

If we were lucky enough to survive this, we would shower quickly, usually in cold water, as the senior cadets had used all the hot water and form a squad in front of the mess hall prior to breakfast, again regardless of weather. A brief inspection might be undertaken if a Senior Cadet felt that it was required. The Junior cadets would wait outside whilst the Seniors assembled at their allotted places inside at the divisional tables. Each division, consisting of thirty cadets was naturally named after famous Naval officers; Philip, Cook, Flinders and Bass. The Divisional Cadet Captain sat at the table head with the other cadets aligned each side in order of seniority.

The junior cadets were required to stand at attention behind their chair and had to request permission to sit. Usually, a senior cadet would ask a naval college related question 'How many steps are there from the marina to the quarterdeck (the oval)?'. Failure to answer correctly resulted in the cadet being obliged to remain standing for a portion of the meal, depending on the whim of the senior cadet. Failure to answer two or more questions correctly could result in more severe penalties, such as the requirement to go immediately to the harbour steps and count them thus missing breakfast. Food, such as it was, was served in order of seniority, sometimes resulting in very paltry servings for those at the bottom of the table. During the meal, the pressure was still on and failure to adhere exactly to culinary standards or excess noise, could result in the cadet eating their meal under the table. The rules were many and immutable. One cadet from our year, Peter Caldwell failed to remove his cap when entering the mess hall. It is an old tradition, which still exists, that Naval Officers entering a room, must remove their caps. The standard punishment is to buy drinks for the whole mess. Poor old Peter had to buy soft drinks for 120 cadets and lost his pay for months as a result. Strangely no other cadet transgressed during my whole time at Creswell.

On completion of the meal, we returned to our cabins to prepare for studies, but the danger was not over. Junior Cadets about to pass through a doorway would need to keep an eye out for any Seniors in the vicinity. The presence of a Senior required the Cadet to stand at attention beside the doorway, take off his cap and await the passage of the Senior Cadet. Third Class, or little snotties, were known for their sneaky ways and would often hide in waiting, hoping to catch a junior unawares before doling out punishment.

The class system even extended to the daily journeys between the accommodation and study blocks (located each side of the Quarterdeck/Oval). Senior Class Cadets were allowed to cross the quarterdeck directly, sauntering along the grass with an air of superiority and privilege. Second Class Cadets could not use the direct route and were obliged to march around the road. Class 3 were required to form a squad and march around but the deprived fourth class would have to double (run) in a squad. Sloppiness often required the squad to repeat the journey (in both directions).

Divisions were held at 10:00am on Sundays. The whole college would assemble on the parade ground (another name for the oval) having spent most of the morning spit polishing boots, polishing brass and blancoing belts and gaiters. The duty guard had to clean rifles or swords contributing to the onerous work of cleaning things.

15. Naval College

Spit polishing the boots was an interesting activity. Some cadets just did not possess the quality of phlegm required for the mandatory mirror finish and would offer favours (my sticky bun at stand easy) to cadets better equipped in the oral fluid area.

There was some free time, Sunday afternoon, but we spent most of that ensuring our gear was ready for the next week

The severity of punishments depended on the seniority of the disciplining cadet and the magnitude of the offence. The most common punishments were the 'decks' (around the quarterdeck) executed at the breaks or occasionally at mealtimes. More heinous crimes such as allowing your pyjamas to peak out of your laundry bag (Scran bag) resulted in punishments meted out by the Cadet Captains or Officers. I received the relatively mild punishment of one day of number nines for this offence. The two worst punishments were Stoppage of Leave and Number Nines. Cadets were not allowed outside of the college during term time except for sporting or other approved events, but stoppage of leave included extra duty and so was to be avoided as it meant that the offending cadet was confined to the college at term breaks. 'Number Nines' was a more serious matter and was doled out in durations of one to ten days.

Immediately after study the punishment squad would assemble. The squad would then be obliged to carry out the kind of drills that the reader may have seen on some of the American marine movies. You know the kind of thing, carrying a rifle at high port that is horizontally above the shoulders and doubling up sand hills. This would be followed by two hours of the most unpleasant work that could be dreamt up by the duty seniors. Cleaning the Heads (toilets) with a toothbrush, careening the bottom of a boat of various sea creatures with an ordinary knife were just two of the imaginative tortures miscreants were subjected to.

On the plus side the humiliating custom of 'slippering' was outlawed during my first year at the college. The victim of this punishment would be ordered to report to a senior cadet's cabin, made to bend over a chair, and subjected to a severe beating with the senior cadet's footwear, not always his slippers.

The stress imposed on Cadets was not accidental. The theory was that if you were to lead men, you had to be both physically and mentally tough. Cadet midshipmen particularly junior cadets were subject to constant discipline, from Petty Officers barking in your ear during drill to an obnoxious dressing down by Senior cadets, both of which had to be stoically borne. The only time you could relax was that heavenly period from lights out at 10:00pm to 5am 'Wakey Wakey' the next morning.

These punishments however, pale into insignificance compared to the experience suffered by one Cadet Midshipman, who was 'cashiered' out of the Navy.

The constant anxiety would occasionally result in mental breakdown and force cadets to do things that they would not normally consider. One such Cadet from the year below me determined that escape or the serious offence of 'Absence without Leave' in Naval Terms, was his only option.

It is difficult to imagine the rationale of his behaviour in these times of enlightenment. He stole two books of some historical value from the College Library, hitched a ride to the nearest town, Nowra, and attempted to sell the books to pay for his rail ticket home. He was caught, returned to the college, arraigned before his fellow cadets and ceremonially divested of his symbols of rank before being cashiered out of the Navy.

The gymnasium, where this excruciating event took place, was also the place where one of the most heroic events of my Naval Career took place. The hero was not a bronzed Australian champion with a square jaw and hardened teak like body but Sidney Lemon, a near sighted rather overweight lump of a lad from Queens Park in Sydney's Eastern Suburbs.

The event was the finale of the College Boxing Tournament. There were only two cadets who qualified for the heavyweight division, Sidney because of his large rotund body shape, and Mick Harrison, a hard man from Leichardt in Sydney's West.

15. Naval College

Mick was a renowned pugilist who had grown up on the streets and who was called 'The Enforcer' in the football team.

It was the biggest mismatch in College History. Sidney was to go five three-minute rounds with Mick and nobody in the college could imagine him lasting to the end of the first round. But he did. Mick attacked as only he knew with a flurry of blows aimed at the solar plexus. Perhaps Sidney's body mass helped him but he stood firm and went for five rounds never landing a punch but still on his feet.

Mick's frustration during the latter stages of the so-called fight was evident as he vainly attempted to land the knockout blow with a series of uppercuts to Sidney's jaw. Mick won the fight of course and he retained his reputation as the college tough guy. Correspondingly, we admired Sidney as a guy who kept on going against all odds.

Recently I spoke to Mick at our 50-year reunion. He explained that, due to the obvious disparity in boxing competence, he had been 'requested' to go easy on Sidney. I prefer my version of events.

Another significant sporting event on the college's calendar was the annual Rugby match between the College first XV and the 'Seadogs', midshipmen who had left the college the previous year. The match was always bruising and keenly fought. The first XV, with the benefit of practice and many matches together, had a significant advantage in teamwork and cohesion and the seadogs the motivation to beat the upstarts and display their seniority.

The year I played for the seadogs, in my second year at University, was a particularly violent affair and Rugby was a poor second. Frustrations on both sides of the game were heightened by constant niggling and harassment but personally I think the poor standard of the game contributed.

Towards the end of the match, the first XV full back, a snobby and supercilious individual, who had taunted us throughout the match, burst from the pack with only a forward between him and the try line. Unfortunately for him, the forward was one Gary Brown, an uncomplicated but emotional character who was known for his direct approach.

The fullback nonchalantly attempted an overconfident sidestep but Gary was having none of it and planted one of the best right-hand jabs ever seen on the fullback's jaw. The event was witnessed by the entire college, including the officers and their wives.

As a consequence, the entire team was subjected to a week of extra drill. Most of the team thought it was worth it and even though Gary's actions resulted in punishment for the whole team, he was not blamed.

The reader will have guessed that the Naval College was steeped in tradition attributable to the British Navy of the nineteenth century and despite the harsh discipline, there were some rather quaint customs.

Occasionally, selected Senior cadets would be asked to an officer's home to look after their children (To babysit would be demeaning) or indulge (a good word given the culinary standard of the college) in afternoon tea. I was particularly lucky having established a good relationship with the Anglican Minister, Reverend Edgar Rolfe. We shared a love of classical music, and his daughter, Susan who was studying at the Conservatorium of Music in Sydney. In case you are wondering, all the commas are in the right place. I spent many a happy hour singing my favourite music as Susan accompanied me on the piano.

But I digress, cadets who were lucky enough to experience these pleasures were expected to write very formalised thank you letters which for some reason were called 'Bread and Butter Letters'.

Bread and Butter letters were mandatory and failure to write one was considered a gross dereliction of duty. I have concocted a letter to demonstrate their obligatory 19th century formality. The words in italics have been added as my attempt at humour.

My time at Naval college was in some ways the best and the worst of life. Once a cadet reached the senior level, life was fairly good. Only the Officers posed any disciplinary threat and they took a very hands-off approach. At least every second weekend was spent off base if you were good enough to make the first XV or first XI. Either way, I look back fondly on those times and, as they say, they were definitely character building.

A 'Bread and Butter' Letter:

Royal Australian Naval College
HMAS Creswell
Jervis Bay
Australian Capital Territory
19:00, Friday 17th May 1968

Dear Lieutenant Smith,

It was a great privilege to look after your well-behaved children yesterday evening (the little brats) and I am pleased to report that their behaviour and general demeanour was excellent and a credit to their parents. (even though they found the chocolate that you left for me and spewed it all over my dress uniform) I enjoyed the opportunity to relax in front of the television whilst studying for my navigation exam (a lie) and I particularly enjoyed Mrs Smith's homemade cakes (They gave a new meaning to the phrase rock cakes and tasted as if they had been burnt several years ago and left to fester in the baking sun (pun)- I had to dismember them into small undetectable pieces with a carving knife before I threw them out)

I look forward with great anticipation to the opportunity to provide this service in the future (No I don't. We had organised a good slippering last night and I missed out on the fun)

I remain your obedient servant (Only because you are an officer)

Septimus Archangel

Cadet Midshipman, RAN

16

University

In December 1968, after almost a year at The Royal Australian Naval College, Jervis Bay, we were sent for our first home leave. That was the one disadvantage of being in the Navy. We only got four weeks a year leave and couldn't enjoy the extended break of University students so in early January 1969, we returned to Sydney to learn about trades, prior to continuing our studies at the University of New South Wales.

We were sent to HMAS Nirimba at Quakers Hill in the outer suburbs of Sydney, the Navy's equivalent to TAFE. The laudable objective was to give us 'Snotties' (Midshipmen) some idea of the tasks that that we would have to delegate to our sailors. As I found out later when at sea, 'delegate' really meant 'stay out of my way. I will call you if I need you.'

The experience was very educational. We were taught how to weld, how to file a cylinder of mild steel so that it was perfectly flat (yes manually file it), and many other trade skills. We also learnt about electrical wiring standards which were not taught at University.

After six weeks we entered university colleges to continue our Degrees.

The first hurdle to overcome in my initial year at Naval College, had been to survive the discipline. The second was to successfully complete first year University. Ironically, the challenge for the second year at my university college was not to be too distracted by the social life in order to pass second year Uni.

Half our year had continued at Jervis Bay on route to becoming seaman or supply officers. The rest of us would have to complete a degree before being let loose in the real world.

I loved University. Too much in fact! Not the study; which I took for granted and went from High Distinctions in first year to just scraping through as a Bachelor of Engineering (Electrical). But the social life. Ah the social life!!

In 1969, the rigid discipline of Naval College was replaced by the complete laissez faire of a university college.

Unfortunately, we were neither prepared nor warned for this and only three graduated from the University of New South Wales with Engineering Degrees.

We were paid as Junior Naval Officers whereas most University students subsisted on a small allowance or had to work unsocial hours to pay their way through Uni. We swaggered around the campus with the arrogance of nineteen-year olds whose future was to order around lesser humans.

Well some of us did. We had girlfriends, cars, money to go out and no restrictions. We wore 'civvies'. Naval uniforms were only worn on formal occasions or to impress a young lady. Mess undress was guaranteed to attract the girls or at least, that is what we thought. We lived, as my mother would say, 'the life of Reilly'. Reilly was a lucky chap. I confess to suffering from a self-important sense of invincibility but I was saved by a chance meeting in the men's toilets of my college, International House which I shall explain shortly.

International House was the ultimate 'meeting of the minds'.

16. University

The college had an equal proportion of men and women and was further divided into half overseas students and half Australian. Residents were from far flung countries such as Norway, Sudan, Chile and even New Zealand. No first-year students were admitted (except my wife, Lesley whose entry was a clerical error) and many of the residents were post grads. What an atmosphere! It was, and possibly still is, a marvellous place to explore the human condition.

A chance meeting changed my life and involved what was my second encounter with Lesley who I have been married to for forty-five years. I had better explain.

The college residents kept a mattress for the occasional visitor in the cleaner's room located at the back of the men's toilets abutting the courtyard. Why the toilets? The ground floor toilets were rarely used as each floor had excellent facilities.

Have you got it? Illicit Mattress for guests hidden in the Cleaner's room-at the back of the Men's Toilets in the courtyard.

It was against College rules to allow outsiders to stay in the college but the rules were often ignored. Lesley had a girlfriend staying with her overnight and we ran into each other as she dragged the communal mattress from its hiding place and I was... well you know why I was there.

We had a brief completely natural conversation which did not include why we were both in the men's toilets. I sheepishly suggested, almost as an afterthought, that we should continue to converse later that evening.

I had first observed Lesley some months previously, when on her first evening in college, she entered the dining room with her friend Rosalind. Rosalind was blond and particularly good looking but I had eyes only for her beautiful red-haired companion in the purple knitted dress. It may seem a bit like a romance novel (not the toilet location of course) that such an encounter could lead to a forty odd year relationship but if you believe in fate, I can affirm that I can remember every detail of her appearance.

Back to the toilet, well not the toilet, but later that evening. The evening was special to me as I sang at the International House Variety Show. I played Toad of Toad Hall in a scene from 'Wind in the Willows', a tour de force that ranks alongside Olivier's Hamlet as a significant moment in the history of theatre. Later, I was accompanied on the organ by the Dean of the College, Prof Willis as I sang 'ol man river' and as a finale, joined my good friend Albert Avolio in a hearty rendition of 'The Bold Gendarmes duet'. It was my almost perfect night. Lots of performing and lots of social interaction.

'O joy O delight, O bliss O beep beep' as Toad would say.

After the concert, I had the temerity to 'cut in' on Lesley and her friend. We danced the night away as the saying goes. After the evening concluded, we retired to the common room, a much more intimate room, where Lesley and I danced to a local radio station (2UW I think) oblivious to those around us.

The meeting in the common room irreversibly changed my life (for the better). Had it been filmed, it would be in that amber filtered sepia with black wavy surrounds.

My emotions surrounding that time are indescribable so I will not try. Suffice to say, it is a memory that will never fade.

17
Fleet Manoeuvres

*W*hat follows is a couple of anecdotes that exemplify of my time at sea after graduating from University, in my case as a Bachelor of Electrical Engineering majoring in Computers and Communications

My first posting, along with three of my colleagues, was to HMAS Melbourne, the Naval Flagship and only Aircraft Carrier.

We were promoted to Sub Lieutenant but as this is the lowest Officer Rank, we were under no illusions as to our status and potential usefulness.

We were correct. The Weapons Electrical Engineering Officer (WEEO), Commander Necrasov was old school. We started at the bottom, carrying out the duties of an able seaman electrical, before progressing to Petty Officer responsibilities. Yet another huge change for us. At University we had learned how to design radar sets, build programs in machine code and the like. My first job on Melbourne was replacing the myriad of light bulbs on the ship.

When 'promoted' to a Petty Officer role, I had the responsibility to maintain the electrical systems associated with the steam catapult; not a hard job but one that you could not afford to get wrong. If a catapult failure occurred when an Aircraft was launched, it could result in the aircraft ditching in the sea right in the path of 25,000 tons of Aircraft Carrier.

A task that I was assigned to was to replace the commutator in one of the five electrical steam generators that provided electrical power to the ship. There were three of us, a Chief Petty Officer, a Leading Electrician and me, as the dogs body.

The generators were situated in the boiler room, a dimly lit, hot steamy space full of machinery with little room for people to manoeuvre. The boiler room was full of all sorts of machinery as well as the two super-heated steam boilers. The noise was almost painful to the ears. The generators, located at the side of a narrow catwalk directly above the boilers, were large metal cylinders approximately two metres high and one and a half metres in diameter. The commutator (the revolving bit in a direct current generator) required three people to remove it from its casing.

We had worked solidly for eight hours and were reassembling the generator when the Chief Petty Officer shouted at me (You had to shout to be heard) that I could go to dinner. I readily agreed but had a feeling that I had forgotten something.

Dinner in the wardroom required the officer to don 'Mess Undress', a photo of which was included earlier. I showered, a mandatory requirement as anyone who entered the boiler room would immediately be covered with oil, dirt and grime, dressed in my formal shirt, cummerbund, real bow tie (clip-ons were forbidden) and jacket and went to dinner.

I had just started my dinner when Commander Necrasov stormed into the wardroom and ordered me to return to the boiler room. He looked angry. When a senior officer gets angry, the best course of action is to obey immediately.

'I will just go and change into my overalls.' I said to him.

17. Fleet Manoeuvres

Wrong comment. I was told that there was no time to change and just to get down there. It was then that I remembered the something. There was a spanner that I had been using to tighten some of the nuts and I had not seen it when I left for dinner.

The spanner had been inadvertently left inside the generator and when it was restarted a loud grinding noise indicated that something was amiss. Sparks had flown literally in the boiler room and later when the Commander spoke to me in the wardroom. The spanner had caused havoc inside the generator and it would need to be completely reassembled. I owned up to my mistake but was not punished for my error other than being forced to spend another eight hours in the boiler room, complete with bow tie and jacket.

We were kept busy aboard ship as not only did we have to undertake our departmental duties, but we also had to stand watches on the bridge in order to attain our Bridge Watch Keeping Certificate.

On one occasion, I was standing the morning watch (4am to 8am) as Second Officer of the Watch. At the time, there were seven ships steaming in line astern just off Jervis Bay in NSW[9]. HMAS Perth, a guided missile destroyer of 5,000 tons displacement led the way, followed by Melbourne, with one other destroyer, HMAS Brisbane and three 'river' class frigates of 2,500 tons astern. HMAS Supply, a ponderous 15,000-ton tanker brought up the rear. I mention the tonnage of these vessels in order to stress the difficulty in steering thousands of tons of metal around the ocean, with totally different speed and turning capabilities, in a quick and precise way.

The sudden appearance of senior officers on the Bridge is a stressful event for any officer of the watch, but the appearance of the Admiral was positively frightening. He had his own Bridge just below the ship's bridge and was rarely seen outside it. He was accompanied by the Captain, Captain Guy Griffiths, the First Lieutenant and the Navigating Officer. The Admiral had decided to conduct Fleet Manoeuvres, presumably to test the readiness of

---

9. Line Astern means single file in non-Naval terms.

the ships at the least convenient time and he gave only 20 minutes notice for the exercise to begin.

I was anticipating a stealthy retreat to the back of the bridge but for some reason, the captain singled me out to con (steer) the ship during the exercise. The thought of guiding 25,000 tons of ship with 1,000+ personnel aboard, whilst being watched by God (the Captain) and the guy who tells god what to do (The Admiral) was daunting to say the least but strangely perhaps, I relished the opportunity to do something few other people would ever get the chance to do. At least I think that is how I felt as a 22-year-old junior officer.

To put the challenge into perspective, the ships were steaming in what was anachronistically called 'Battle Order' meaning we were steaming as close to one another as Naval regulations would allow, an average of 500 metres between ships. The fleet had been ordered to increase speed and was travelling at 18knots (approximately 33 kph) close to Melbourne's maximum speed. At 18 knots, it would take Melbourne almost 3 kilometres to stop.

The ship had also been brought to the highest state of alert; Condition Zulu. Condition Zulu required the whole crew to take up their allotted Battle stations. All watertight doors were closed turning the ship into potentially hundreds of small metal coffins. This may seem dramatic but there was a serious risk in a collision for those trapped in the bowels of the ship between the open air and several of these metal multi clamped doors. Melbourne had been involved in two collisions, neither of which were her fault but the Navy was extremely sensitive to the potential of collision.

It is hard to describe the atmosphere on the bridge as zero hour for the exercise approached. The exercise would require exemplary teamwork and error free decision making and all this under the critical gaze of the Admiral. We were the football team in the dressing room just before the start of the grand-final. The atmosphere silent but heavily charged. I was in a high state of anxiety. We waited quite literally for the starting gun, a small cannon used for ceremonial occasions, to announce to the fleet that the exercise had started.

17. Fleet Manoeuvres

The Admiral had ordered that the ship movements would be signalled using semaphore, a series of various patterned flags raised in a particular sequence, to communicate orders. Incidentally, this system was used in Lord Nelson's era. He famously issued the order 'England expects everyman to do his duty' by semaphore. We did have some technology in those days but the Admiral reasoned that, in a battle, communications could be jammed or destroyed and the fleet might have to revert to old fashioned ways.

The exercise commenced in somewhat of an anticlimax as the Admiral calmly ordered all ships to undertake a relatively simple manoeuvre and turn together at right angles to our current course. The captain had instructed me to give the appropriate steering and engine orders whilst the first officer of the watch (OOW), Lieutenant Newton, was to monitor the positions of the other ships. His job was much more difficult than mine as he would need to constantly take compass bearings at the binnacle at the front of the bridge and monitor the radar screen at the rear of the Bridge to assess the relative position of the other ships whilst threading his way through the mass of milling senior officers. My job, whilst critical, was relatively simple. My only communication was via a rubberised microphone to the wheelhouse located in the depths of the ship.[10] I would have to anticipate the way the ship would respond to my orders. How much wheel should be ordered? The more rudder is used, the faster the ship would swing but due to a phenomenon called cavitation, ships do not turn in a steady rate. At higher speeds, the water pressure flowing past the rudder can result in low pressure air pockets which reduce the effectiveness of the rudder.

I ordered 'port 30' whilst the OOW relayed positions and bearings of the other vessels. The ships would need to execute a synchronised turn if we were to avoid the ire of the Admiral. The destroyers and

---

10. The wheelhouse was key to the ships survival and was therefore located as far away from the action as possible. Melbourne's wheelhouse was a room of approximately 3 metres square with a large one and a half metre wheel in the centre and a set of telegraphs which signalled the required revolutions of the ship's two enormous steam engines.

frigates were capable of thirty plus knots and compared to the lumbering flagship, they could turn on a sixpence.

You may have seen Naval related movies with heroic young Naval officers dressed in ceremonial attire driving their ships like sports cars, dashing around the ocean with gay abandon.

Our reality was significantly different. The bridge was the size of a small living room, surrounded by electronic displays and other such obstacles. The bridge consisted mainly of bare grey metal with reinforced almost translucent glass windows and was adorned by voice operated telephones, a couple of voice pipes (used for communication to the critical areas of the ship in dire emergencies) and a few unremarkable electrical switches. On this occasion, it was cramped with seven officers and three ratings occupying its grey metal deck space.

There was no room for the movie actor to pace meaningfully around whilst planning his next brilliant tactic. There was only one chair, the captain's chair which was out of bounds to all others. On really quiet watches we would surreptitiously sit in this chair to take a quick breather whilst consuming a mug of strong cocoa (Chai).

Because of its sheer bulk, the ship does not 'answer the helm' immediately and it is several nervous seconds until you feel the ship move almost imperceptibly beneath you. As the ship swings, it gathers momentum and if the turn is significant, in this case 90 degrees, it gathers pace in an alarming manner. The real tricky bit is to bring the ship to the desired bearing by applying the opposite wheel, in my case 'Starboard 10'. As the ship nears the required bearing, the order 'amidships' brings the rudder to its neutral position and if you get it right, the ship will gracefully settle onto its new course. The timing of the orders is critical, especially on a 25,000-ton ship. If an order is given too soon the ship will not reach the new course, too late and she will swing past the bearing.'.

Experienced captains could turn this into a fine art and were known throughout the fleet for their seamanship prowess or lack thereof. Captain Griffiths was one of the best and would sometimes use the engines himself by ordering one engine astern to accelerate the turn. We were turning with relatively agile destroyers and I vaguely recall that he assisted in precisely that manner.

The exercise lasted a tension packed hour as the seven ships turned abreast then back into line or into two columns. Several other formations escape my memory. As the ship turns it sways like an oversized car as the sea resists its changed momentum.

The time flew. There was no opportunity to take a breather and I could not afford even a momentary lapse in concentration. At the end, I was mentally and physically exhausted.

Oh! and did I carry out the task successfully? I can't remember to be honest but I cannot recall any bellowed command countermanding my orders, nor any sense of impending disaster so I guess I must have done ok.

I still marvel at my luck in being given the opportunity to 'drive' the ship as the Admiral put us through our paces. The feeling was almost surreal. Thousands of tons of metal with thousands of sailors aboard turning in unison and me, the second officer of the watch, directing.

As any sailor will tell you, there are many other stories but I will leave those for another occasion.

18

Epilogue

I feel that a summary is required but I have no idea how to end this.

'The hero will return in another exciting episode of ???' I think not.

Perhaps I should go back to the beginning.

My intent was to record a fairly interesting life from the perspective of change. A snotty nosed dirty kneed grammar school kid from the impoverished North of England, travelled to the other end of the world, finished school on a rocket range in the Australian Desert and then became a very seasick Naval Officer and an Engineer.

Everybody has a story.

Appendix A
What is a Ten Pound Pom?

*A*rthur Caldwell was the Minister of Immigration in 1945. He was a staunch advocate of the White Australia Policy and was responsible for implementing the assisted passage scheme.

Caldwell understood the importance of the media and often appeared on government propaganda news reels to manage public perception and fears around White Australia's new immigration policy. He was responsible for hatching a plan to bring a batch of Europeans to Australia. They came in droves from Italy, Greece, the Baltic countries and of course Poms, mainly from the impoverished cities to satisfy the perceived demand for unskilled labour.

In 1946 Caldwell claimed that 'for every foreign migrant there will be ten people from the United Kingdom'. I believe he made this statement to counteract the public's dislike for foreigners. It was expected that English speaking migrants would assimilate more easily than other Europeans. In reality, the differences between the average 'white' Australian and the Britishers gave the lie to this idea. Many of the Poms were fixed in their attitudes and expected a warmer little Britain. There are several versions for the acronym 'POM', some of them unprintable. I will go with 'Prisoner of Mother England.'

Both the Australian and British governments subsidized the Ten Pound Pom scheme, though Britain gradually reduced its contribution to the fare after 1950, down to £150,000 per year (enough to pay for around 1,000 migrants).

Upon arrival in Australia the government organised transit, reception, accommodation and employment for the Ten Pound Poms in holding centres, transit camps and migrant hostels.

The living conditions in the migrant hostels were often poor and jobs were not always available. The marketing campaign in the UK, with its colourful posters and brochures, had been somewhat deceiving! Around a quarter of a million Poms returned home within a few years of arriving in Australia, though many of these subsequently changed their mind and came back to Australia (Boomerang Poms).

The Ten Pound Pom scheme ended in 1972.

Key features of the scheme:

Fares:

- ☐ £10 for adults, hence the name Ten Pound Poms!
- ☐ £5 for children aged 14-18 (free by the 1960s)

In 1952, the normal cost of an adult fare to Australia was £120 and the average male manual worker's weekly wage was around £10.

Appendix A. What is a Ten Pound Pom?

Eligibility Criteria:
- British subjects (including Irish and Welsh)
- Citizens of the Republic of Ireland were also eligible so long as they were born before 1949
- White (mixed race Britons unlikely to be accepted)
- Under 45 (though the scheme was occasionally extended to parents and grandparents)
- In sound health

Conditions:
- Stay 2 years in Australia or refund the balance of the fare (around £120)

Timeline:
- 1947 – Scheme started with a bang (400,000 Poms registered at Australia House)
- 1950 – Britain reduced its contribution to the fare to £25 per adult (around 50%)
- 1951 – Britain limited its contribution to £500,000 per annum
- 1954 – Britain limited its contribution to £150,000 per annum (1,000 migrants)
- 1957 – 'Bring Out a Briton' campaign launched
- 1959 – Nest Egg Scheme launched
- 1969 – Peak year (nearly 80,000 Britons emigrated to Australia)
- 1972 – Assisted passage modified to £75 per migrant.
- 1982 – Assisted Passage Scheme ended

Appendix B
The Barber Line

*I*n the 1840s, gas lighting became a requirement for street lighting for a progressive township. Harrogate Council decided to build a gas works to supply the Gas. The Gas was generated from burning 'coke'. Coke is a coal derivative produced by the destructive distillation of coal. It has less odour than coal and burns more effectively as it contains no water.

The original intention of the Harrogate Gas Company was to build a gas works adjoining the railway at Starbeck. The coal required to manufacture the gas could then be transported by rail directly to the plant. This plan was dropped for reasons that remain a mystery to this day. The alternative site was a long way from the railway beside the Ripon Road at New Park, Bilton. The streets of Harrogate were lit by gas lamps for the first time in February 1848 from gas manufactured and stored at these Gas works. At the time, Bilton was a farming area and therefore remote from the dignitaries who lived in Harrogate proper. The Farmers had no say in the matter. The smelly noisy gasworks were built in the middle of a farm in Bilton.

The coal had to be transported from the railhead at Starbeck originally by horse and cart and from 1871 by a number of steam road locomotives which were routed through High Harrogate (The posh area). and then out to Bilton.

This led to a number of complaints to the gas company arising from the amount of noise and smoke this generated especially when coal was being transported through the night.

To combat this and to alleviate to cost of transporting coal for four miles through the streets of Harrogate, the companies agreed to open a coal yard at Bilton Junction just where the railway to Ripon crossed Bilton Lane. The distance to the Gasworks, across farming land was a mere two miles and nowhere near the town.

This was in 1880 and, though the shorter road route helped with both the transport and environmental problems, it was not an ideal solution as coal still had to be transported by cart the two miles to the Gasworks.

Plans were then made for a narrow-gauge railway to carry the coal direct from Bilton Junction to New Park and construction work began in the spring of 1907.

The gas company purchased its first locomotive in 1908 which it named 'Barber' after the chairman of the gas company. The line included a tunnel which carried the tracks under much of New Park and Skipton Road and was officially opened in December 1908.

Changes in the way that gas was produced and the fact that even during the 1950s a large proportion of the coal was still being transported by road led to the decision in September 1955 to close the line and the last train passed through the New Park tunnel in July 1956.

By the end of 1965, the Harrogate Gas works had been completely converted to the storage of natural gas and both the narrow-gauge railway and the gas production plant it supplied had gone.

Appendix B. The Barber Line

Today the railway is somewhat overgrown and the tracks have long been removed but with the use of a little imagination it is still possible to make out the position of the Bilton yard and the two levels where the coal was tipped from the main line into wagons waiting to take it to the New Park gas works.

Appendix C
A Brief History of Yorkshire

Introduction

Unnecessary as whatever appears here will be repeated in the text.

Geography

Yorkshire is an isolated country bounded by:

- ☐ A mighty river to the South; The Humber, which is mighty for about 10 miles
- ☐ A not so mighty river to the North; The Tees which at least separates Yorkshire from the barbarians to the North)
- ☐ A frozen sea to the east; The North Sea-It is not actually frozen, but you try jumping in it and you will be.
- ☐ A mighty mountain range to the west (actually a gentle sloping hill), The Pennines, which keeps Lancastrians out.

Yorkshire's main exports were Coal, Wool and Michael Parkinson (though he keeps coming back).

Yorkshire is separated into two parts, the south where miners live and the north where farmers live.

Farmers are no nonsense folk who like sheep because they don't take much to look after and who speak only when there is no alternative (The farmers not the sheep). They usually live in the Dales which are pleasant little valleys with pleasant little meandering rivers that go nowhere outside Yorkshire. The sheep live on the moors which are the hills above the dales. Farmers don't bother with leisure because it sounds like fun and fun is for Sissies, as is leisure.

Miners live in little stone villages next to slag heaps and are incredibly sad people because they either work or don't work.

Entertainment in these villages is provided by a brass band which consists of unemployed miners.

Yorkshire folk speak of places outside of Yorkshire as 'The South' or Lancashire. The bosses come from the South. Lancashire is populated by people who want to live in Yorkshire but are prevented from doing so by the immigration laws. You can always tell people from Lancashire because their language is completely different and because they cannot wear a flat cap properly.

It is believed that there is somewhere north of the Tees but as nobody from Yorkshire has ever been there, and therefore, just like the great southland, it is not considered as 'a place'

Weather

Yorkshire has two seasons. Winter lasts for eleven months and a few days and is one of the reasons that Yorkshire folk are known for their toughness and stoicism. Summer is usually a day in August when it does not rain, sleet or snow.

Language

The Yorkshire language is best described by the phrase, 'Beautiful yet simple' as is the rest of Yorkshire's unique culture

It is derived from English, though Yorkshire people would claim the opposite. The Yorkshire dialect uses only meaningful words and just like Latin, another language derived from Yorkshire, disposes of such unnecessary elements as prepositions and conjunctions. For example, 'Would you please close the door?' has many of these unnecessary elements such as 'would you please', 'the' and a question mark. The speaker requires the door closed so the question mark is superfluous as is the 'you' bit. Who else would they be speaking too and anyway they don't care who closes the door? The sentence is more meaningful and efficient when minimised to 'Put wood in't 'oil'.

The Yorkshire language does not require superfluous phrases to explain how the speaker is feeling. If the tone is loud, they are angry and need immediate adherence. If it is soft, they are about to engage in activities that really should not be spoken about.

Sport

There are only two sports regularly played in Yorkshire, Cricket and Rugby League. These are quintessential Yorkshire sports and, of course were both invented in Yorkshire.

A couple of other sports have been tried but have not really taken on.

In 2014, there was a cycle race around the dales which caught a lot of attention, but it was discontinued after it was discovered that a lot of bicycles were cluttering up the countryside and that it was invented 'down south'

Another sport that used to be played in Yorkshire is 'Premier League Soccer' Participation in this sport was very popular at one stage but it became a game for 'Sissies' and attracted too many rules (see Rugby League) so Yorkshire Teams withdrew from the competition to play in a much more realistic competition called 'The Championship'. 'Scouting' teams from Yorkshire's extremities, such as Hull City and Middlesbrough, are occasionally sent to the Premier League to look for improvement but, after one season, they tend to become disenchanted and return to the real stuff.

Cricket

Cricket is a game that the uninitiated believe is based on running between two lots of sticks and scoring what are termed 'runs'. This notion is entirely false as exemplified by the great Geoff Boycott.

Cricket is about spending as much time in the Sun or drizzle as you can, in order to enjoy the ambience and the frustration of the lad with the ball at the other end who wants to kill you. The bat is only used when the ball is likely to hit the stumps and can usually be ignored.

Incidentally, there are those who still dispute the decision by the Yorkshire Cricket Board in 1985 to allow people born outside the country to play for Yorkshire. It is not all bad though as a Yorkshire team composed mainly of Australians, won the county championship in 2014.

Rugby League

Rugby League is another contribution to world peace that was invented in Yorkshire. It was noticed that after a few pints in the pub, a few of the lads would get cranky and have a bit of a barney. This was not good for the locals as there was a risk that their beer would be spilt so they told the lads to go and play outside and hence Rugby League was invented.

At some later stage, a ball was introduced but even today, this could be discounted as superfluous. The game ends, as in the past, when one team is too exhausted to continue, when the teams want to go back to the pub for a 'roady' or when one of the wives gets cranky and drags the star prop back home to look after the kids.

Appendix C. A Brief History of Yorkshire

Famous People

Geoff Boycott – English Cricketer

Boycott epitomises the Yorkshire spirit. His 'only score when there is nothing else to do' attitude is supplemented by a steely desire to enjoy the environment as long as possible.

Freddie Truman – Also an English Cricketer

Freddie or Sir Freddie as he is known down South, was a fast bowler of international repute. i.e. outside of Yorkshire. As a true Yorkshireman, Freddie did not concern himself with the fineries of swing and seam or other unnecessary concerns. His motivation was to eliminate the guy at the other end because they were not from Yorkshire. He is also reputed to have been a good storyteller.

Sean Bean – Actor

Seen is only just a Yorkshireman as he comes from South Yorkshire, but he was born within the borders and is famous, so he rates a mention. His 'say what you mean and mean what you say' approach to acting has a certain Yorkshire resonance although comparisons with Sir Lawrence Olivier are completely inappropriate as Sir Lawrence did not come from Yorkshire and was nowhere near as good.

Culture

Yorkshire's unique culture has survived for hundreds of years because Yorkshire people don't see any reason to change or travel outside the country, despite the invasions from other countries, including England.

This is best summed up by the famous Hale and Pace skit 'Yorkshire Airlines' when Captain Boycott leaves Leeds International Airport only to return 20 minutes later because 'Why the bloody 'ell would you want to go outside Yorkshire'

Literature

Literature in Yorkshire is like its inhabitants, simple yet beautiful. Compare if you will, the following quotations from a famous southerner, Jane Austen and the Bronte sisters. Austen from a background of privilege and station and the Bronte Sisters from a typical Yorkshire village, Haworth. The Bronte's were the daughters of a no-nonsense country vicar. Haworth is a stone village with stone streets and stone scenery where niceties like flowers are removed from view because they impede the landscape.

Jane Austen Quote from 'Persuasion.' The quotation speaks for itself; full of flowery language and cluttered with unnecessary dialogue.

"I can listen no longer in silence. I must speak to you by such means as are within my reach. You pierce my soul. I am half agony, half hope. Tell me not that I am too late, that such precious feelings are gone for ever. I offer myself to you again with a heart even more your own than when you almost broke it, eight years and a half ago. Dare not say that man forgets sooner than woman, that his love has an earlier death. I have loved none but you. Unjust I may have been, weak and resentful I have been, but never inconstant. You alone have brought me to Bath. For you alone, I think and plan. Have you not seen this? Can you fail to have understood my wishes? I had not waited even these ten days, could I have read your feelings, as I think you must have penetrated mine. I can hardly write.......etc. etc.

Typical southerner- makes one sentence into several paragraphs and still doesn't get to the point.

The Bronte's

'Heathcliff'…. 'Cathy'.

Two people in love running towards each other but as it is likely that they already know each other's names even these two words are redundant.

Cuisine

Fish and Chips

Fish and chips were invented in Yorkshire. Halibut became a staple diet when people outside of Yorkshire refused to eat it. Yorkshire folk not wanting to waste good food or spend excessive time preparing it, threw it in the frying pan with a bit of left-over beer and flour.

But it was not enough. People knew that any good meal required vegetables. This problem was solved when a farmer with too many spuds (potatoes) became frustrated and attacked the potatoes with his spade. He was so angry in fact that he had to go to the pub to calm down. In his absence, his wife discovered the surplus spuds that looked like wood chips and threw them in the frying pan for tea and Fish and Chips were born.

Fish and chips became the staple diet, but people wanted more. It was inconvenient to do full roast dinners when on holiday in Scarborough, Bridlington (Brid) or Redcar (Yorkshire holiday towns) and fish and chips seemed the obvious solution. You did not need lengthy preparation or fine cutlery to eat Fish and Chips. The problem was plates.

Even this problem was solved in typical Yorkshire fashion when one young lady who had travelled down south (the reason for her visit is unclear) observed that people were reading newspapers and then throwing them away. Again, the solution was obvious, import the old newspapers and use them as plates. To this day, you can see Yorkshire folk walking along the pier on holiday and eating fish and chips wrapped in newspaper.

Yorkshire Pudding

Yorkshire pudding was created as a fill in between the pub and Sunday lunch and is therefore a kind of entrée as the Southerners call it. In fact, when a roast is not available due to lack of brass[11],

---

11. Brass = Money

Yorkshire Pudding becomes the main course. Gravy is optional and mint sauce can be added for those with a refined palette. Social status in Yorkshire is measured by the quality of your Yorkshire pudding.

National Anthem

The Yorkshire National anthem reflects the Yorkshire culture and spirit. It is called 'On Ilkla Moor Baht at' ('On Ilkley Moor without a hat'); and is about people dying from a cold because they don't have a hat on and then being eaten by their colleagues eating themselves via worms and ducks.

The national poem requires no introduction, though it may need translation, and is reproduced below:

> *'Ear all, see all, say nowt;*
> *Eyt all, sup all, pay nowt;*
> *And if ivver tha does owt fer nowt –*
> *Allus do it fer thissen.*[12]

The poem ironically does an injustice to the people of Yorkshire. Though it is often said that a Yorkshireman is a Scotsman with all the generosity squeezed out of him, this is a long way from the truth. Yorkshire people may be a bit coy with outsiders but once you get to know them, they would give you all they have, which is usually not much. (but it is the thought that counts)

Conclusion

Unnecessary.

---

12. 'Hear all, see all, say nothing; Eat all, drink all, pay nothing; And if ever you do anything for nothing – always do it for yourself

Appendix D
A Brief History of Woomera

Beginnings

*I*n the late 1940s, Britain was a major contender in the blossoming (pun intended) arms race. Russia and the USA were major beneficiaries of the technological spoils of war from the defeated Germany. The V2 rockets, once intended to flatten London would now be used as a blueprint for a new era of missile development. The UK had combined its atomic knowledge with the superior German technology and was competing with the soon to be superpowers to develop an atomic bomb. England did not have the vast deserts and tundra of the US and Russia and therefore looked to its former colonies to provide the space to flex its military muscle. A large, remote area in which to test new weapons systems was essential.

Various sites were considered in a number of countries, including one in Canada. In the end, Australia's enormous virtually unpopulated interior won the day, and the *Long-Range Weapons Establishment* (Woomera rocket range) came into existence on 1 April 1947 as a joint project between Britain and Australia.

Ironically, 'Woomera' is the aboriginal word for the spear launching device used by desert aborigines. Woomera was launched (second intended pun).

Some months later, a party of surveyors was despatched from Adelaide to find a suitable location for the soon to be 'Long Range Weapons Establishment'. How odd they must have seemed, dressed in military khaki, shorts and pith helmets with their theodolites, noisy Land Rovers and white ridgepole tents.

They selected a spot near the Pimba settlement because it was close to the railway and the track to Alice Springs with the grandiose name of 'The Sturt Highway' and because there was some semblance of vegetation located in a small hollow where stockmen could occasionally get water. They had found a location with 2 possible transportation facilities and one of the few almost green areas, in thousands of kilometres of gibber plain.

Woomera Village in the 1960s

The village was unique and impervious to outsiders and developed its own persona. A Woomerite would discuss the condition of the Port Road, the dirt road connecting Woomera to civilisation; vociferously discuss Woomera's football or cricket competition and the local scandals. Many of the inhabitants had a family elsewhere and the seclusion and non-permanent nature of the village encouraged some to stray from the moral path.

The track to Port Augusta was infamous. The extra wear and tear generated by traffic from Woomera and the increasing number of road trains travelling to and from Alice Springs could result in major breakdowns or unplanned trips into the donga. The dusty gibber plain and sand dunes invaded the surface or exposed large tracks of rock. The once a year deluge of rain could turn the road into an unnavigable swamp. Discussions on the state of the 'Port Road' often took precedence over current affairs (Unless of course they were affairs of Woomera residents). To be a resident of Woomera amidst the harshness of the desert landscape and separated from the rest of 'civilisation' was an experience that few were lucky enough to share.

A curious tourist would have no chance of getting past the well patrolled guard gate and even family and friends of residents had to submit to an exhaustive three-month security check before being allowed into the village.

The isolation was reinforced by the dubious transport options available: if the public service and army types returning to the Weapons Research Establishment in Adelaide were prepared to give up a seat, a resident could fly to Adelaide on one of the ancient DC3s or Bristol freighters. Alternatively, you could risk the 480-kilometre car journey to Adelaide via the infamous Port Road or wait a week or so for 'The Bud' a single carriage diesel train that traversed the 500 km trip to Adelaide in about seven hours.

The village was a microcosm of a cosmopolitan city. It boasted

- ☐ An Olympic size pool (A second pool and diving pool were built later)
- ☐ An air-conditioned theatre,
- ☐ Five sporting ovals, three of which were grass.
- ☐ A golf course (which admittedly had browns rather than greens and was plagued by racing goannas who often mistook golf balls for birds' eggs and disappeared into the bush at speeds that even a four-wheel drive had trouble matching)
- ☐ Catholic, Anglican, Uniting and Lutheran Churches built from slate brick and granite and a strong Jewish sect
- ☐ Over 70 clubs including archaeological, tennis, model aircraft clubs
- ☐ Three messes organised along army lines (junior, staff and senior) A fourth mess was reserved for the employees of the European Launcher Development Organisation (ELDO) and an RSL. The ELDO Mess has now been converted into a hotel for visitors

- ☐ A zoo (the arboretum), which boasted an albino wombat as its prize exhibit.
- ☐ A school of nearly 800 students (K1-K12)- (sorry seven ovals and three grass)
- ☐ A town hall and its own newspaper, 'The Gibber Gabber' which was started during the first few weeks of Woomera's existence in 1947 and is still going strong today.

The village was scaled down in the seventies and today less than 150 hardy souls populate the village. The remaining Woomerites still reminisce about their dynamic past and dream of a return to the time when Woomera was at the forefront of technology and Woomera residents considered themselves as the chosen few, cloistered in modern monastic spiritualism.

Woomera could have been Australia's first space station and in fact satellites were launched from Woomera but Robert Menzies displaying a surprising lack of vision, didn't think the space race would take off (another pun sorry) and the development that could have made Woomera into a major space centre never took place.

ELDO

The longest and most expensive project in Woomera's history was the European Launcher Development Organisation's (ELDO) Europa project designed to launch a series of 'commercially viable' satellites into space.

The rocket was constructed of a British first stage, French second stage, a German third stage, an Italian satellite and Dutch guidance systems. It was an experiment in technological multiculturalism and dominated activity at Woomera for several years. Seven trials were conducted, the last two designed to launch a satellite into orbit but alas the project didn't achieve its ambitious goal until moved to French Guiana in the 1980s.

It is a little-known fact that Australia was the fourth country to successfully launch a satellite into orbit after USA, USSR and Europe. The propulsion system was a second-hand USA missile, a Redstone rocket, purchased from NASA. Australia launched two satellites into orbit in November 1967. This put Australia ahead of China, Japan and several other major countries in the space race. A bronze medal for the Lilliputians but no cigar for the Australian government. The sky could figuratively not be the limit but Federal inertia meant lost opportunity.

The satellite, with its third stage rocket motor still attached, was placed in a near-polar orbit.

The first satellite re-entered over the Atlantic Ocean west of Ireland at 11:34 GMT on 10 January 1968. It had completed 642 orbits and transmitted scientific data for 73 orbits.

The first stage of the launch vehicle fell in the Simpson Desert of central Australia, while the second stage came down in the Gulf of Carpentaria. Little of the second stage would have survived re-entry. However, the first stage was recovered in April 1990 and returned to Woomera some 600 kilometres south.

The WRESAT project followed on from an existing program of upper atmospheric research using sounding rockets. The satellite was developed by the then Weapons Research Establishment (Salisbury,

South Australia) and the Department of Physics at the University of Adelaide in South Australia. The project took less than a year from concept to launch. The Redstone launch vehicle was left over from the SPARTA project - a joint U.S.-U.K.-Australian research program aimed at understanding re-entry phenomena.

www.ingramcontent.com/pod-product-compliance
Lightning Source LLC
Chambersburg PA
CBHW021150080526
44588CB00008B/281